GOLF

MISTAKES

& How
to Correct
Them

Oliver Heuler

Sterling Publishing Co., Inc.
New York

Translated by Elisabeth E. Reinersmann

Library of Congress Cataloging-in-Publication Data
Heuler, Oliver.
    [Fehler & Korrekturen.   English]
    Golf mistakes & how to correct them / Oliver Heuler.
        p.   cm.
    Includes index.
    ISBN 0-8069-0301-5
    1. Golf.   I. Title.
  GV965.H436   1997
  796.352—dc21
                                                97-21598
                                                CIP

10   9   8   7   6   5   4   3   2

Published 1997 by Sterling Publishing Company, Inc.
387 Park Avenue South, New York, N.Y. 10016
Originally published by Falken-Verlag GmbH
under the title *Fehler & Korrekturen*
© 1996 by Falken-Verlag GmbH, 65527 Niedernhausen/Ts
English translation © 1997 Sterling Publishing Co., Inc.
Distributed in Canada by Sterling Publishing
c/o Canadian Manda Group, One Atlantic Avenue, Suite 105
Toronto, Ontario, Canada M6K 3E7
Distributed in Great Britain and Europe by Cassell PLC
Wellington House, 125 Strand, London WC2R 0BB, England
Distributed in Australia by Capricorn Link (Australia) Pty Ltd.
P.O. Box 6651, Baulkham Hills, Business Centre, NSW 2153, Australia
Printed in Hong Kong

Sterling ISBN 0-8069-0301-5

CONTENTS

INTRODUCTION

Your golf game is not improving. For months, everything has seemed to be at a standstill. In some ways, things have even become worse over time. Still, you dislike the idea of having to start all over again and of learning a new swing, and the idea of making changes just for the sake of following some teaching method is even less appealing.

Actually, you don't have to start all over again or learn a new swing. You should correct your swing only when the result of the change improves your swing and makes it simpler. Corrections that are only noticeable after years of training are useless for the amateur golfer. To achieve quick results and improvements, you need to correct individual aspects of your game.

Since a golf instructor is not always available, you need to be able to help yourself, and that is possible even if you can't observe yourself. You can learn to interpret the flight of the ball by understanding the law that governs its flight and by understanding the factors involved at the moment of impact. You won't need a golf instructor's extensive knowledge in order to learn this. You'll

only need the information that is important for your golf swing.

Because several factors are usually involved in each mistake, you must analyze the shots that always seem to produce a particular mistake. For instance, if you slice the ball when you use a wood and your short swings always veer off to the left, the corrections you need to make are totally different from the corrections you'd need to make if your short shots moved straight to the right.

Therefore, every discussion about the reasons for a mistake begins with a list of the faulty shots that might accompany it. This system will help you to quickly discover the reasons for your problems. The suggested exercises will help you correct those problems.

Discover how quickly you can improve your swing using this book. You'll find all the information you need, right here, to correct your mistakes and improve your game.

ANALYZING MISTAKES

All mistakes are the result of faults that occur at the moment of impact. Knowing something about the law that governs the flight of a ball provides the information you need to make corrections.

In order for a ball to fly straight to the target, the clubface must point precisely in the direction of the target at the moment of impact. The most important factor is the position of the clubface at the moment of impact.

The horizontal angle at impact influences the initial direction the ball will take.

The position of the clubface influences the direction of the ball and the spin of the ball. For instance, if the clubface points either to the right or to the left at the moment of impact, the ball will start out in that direction. During its flight, the ball will veer even more strongly in that direction.

At the moment of impact, if the heel of the club is higher above the ground than the tip of the club, the effect will be the same, although to a some-

what lesser degree, as if you turned the clubface to the right.

In addition, the clubface must approach the ball according to its loft. This means that at the moment of impact the grip of the club should not be too far behind or too far ahead of the ball; otherwise the curve of flight will be either too high or too flat.

The angle of the club determines the direction in which the club will move at the moment of impact. This angle has two components. First, at the moment of impact, the club must be moving in the direction of the target and must not swing to the left or to the right, or the ball will start off in the wrong direction. And second, the club must not move up or down too steeply since this would change the optimum start, the height during flight, and the backspin.

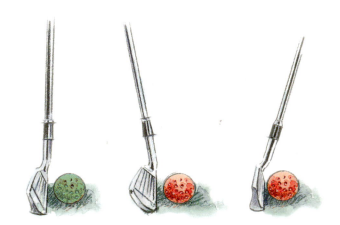

The loft of the club at the moment of impact influences the start of the flight and the height of the ball during flight (above) *and the lie of the direction in which the clubface points* (below)*.*

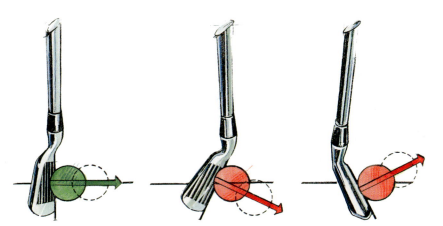

The position of the clubface at the moment of impact is the most important factor in determining the initial direction the ball takes and the direction of the spin.

ANALYZING MISTAKES

The vertical angle at the moment of impact influences the way the ball starts out and the height of the flight.

The optimal energy transfer takes place when you hit the ball with the sweet spot of the club. If you hit the ball too high or too low or if you hit the ball with the heel or the tip at the moment of impact, the club will rotate in your hands. The result is a great loss of energy which shortens the flight of the ball.

The speed of the clubhead at the moment of impact is an important factor in determining how far the ball will fly, but it is not the only factor. Even if the clubhead is travel-ing with high speed, the distance will be considerably reduced if other factors are wrong at the moment of impact.

These factors are the key to a successful golf game. In order to improve your game, you need to find out how far you deviate from the ideal at the moment of impact. The best indicator is the flight of the ball, but in order to interpret this information, you must know something about the laws that govern the flight of a ball.

The optimal transfer of energy from the club to the ball only takes place when you hit the ball with the sweet spot.

Laws Governing the Flight of a Ball

A ball can start out in one of three directions: to your right (push), to your left (pull), or straight to the target. In order to analyze and correct any of these, you must evaluate the direction of the ball at the start in relation to your position. The direction in which the ball takes off depends on the aim.

For instance, a player positioned too far to the right of the target, who intends to hit straight to the target, really does not hit a straight shot but pulls the ball. Since lining up improperly is the rule rather than the exception, you need to concentrate on positioning yourself properly. After the ball is in the air, you can observe three scenarios: the ball continues off to the right (slice), off to the left (hook), or straight ahead.

The best way to analyze the flight of the ball is for the player to use a club with little loft (wood or long iron). For example, when you hit the ball with a 9 iron, which has 3 degrees of loft, the speed of the clubhead and the low point of impact produce only one-eighth of the sidespin that a driver with the identical loft would produce. Thus, a ball hit with a short iron seldom has a very steep flight curve.

In order to understand how the individual factors at the moment of impact relate to the flight path of a ball, let's assume that you hit the ball with the sweet spot. In practical terms, of course, a ball can also start off to the right and then veer off to the left simply because you hit the ball with the tip of the clubhead.

A ball always veers off to the side when, at the moment of impact, the clubface is not perpendicular to the direction of the swing. Therefore, the initial direction of the ball is always a combination of the direction of the swing and the position of the clubface at the moment of impact. Depending on the speed of the clubhead, the position of the clubface is the dominant factor.

Now let's look at the connection between the position of the clubface and the direction of the swing, which is responsible for a number of individual mistakes.

In the case of a straight shot, the club was moving straight in the direction of the target at the moment of contact, and the clubface was perpendicular to the line of the target.

When you pulled the ball at

ANALYZING MISTAKES

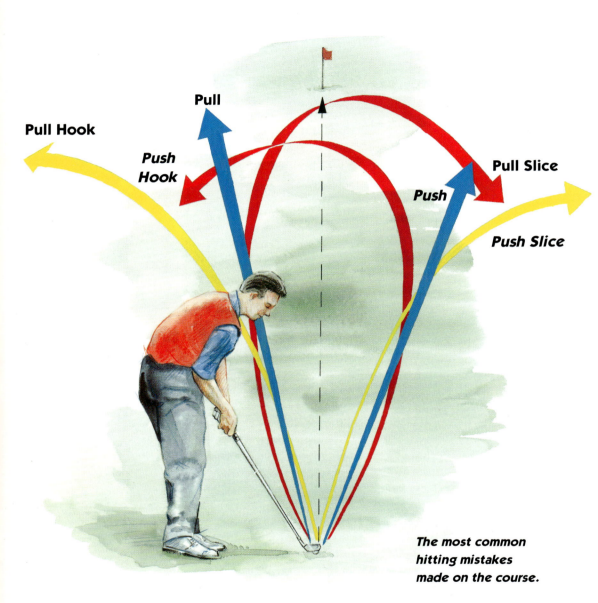

Pull Hook

Pull

Push Hook

Pull Slice

Push

Push Slice

The most common hitting mistakes made on the course.

the moment of impact, the clubhead was moving to the left and crossed the goal line from the outside in. At the moment of impact, the face of the club was perpendicular to the direction of the swing. In other words, the clubface turned to the left of the line to the target. However, when you use a short iron, you can pull a ball simply because you close the clubface, without the club swinging through the ball from the outside in.

You push the ball when, at the moment of impact, the clubhead moves to the right and the face of the club is perpendicular to the direction of the swing. In other words, the clubface turns to the left of the line to the target. With short irons and with clubheads moving with minimal speed, you can push through the ball with an open clubface without the club swinging through the ball from inside out.

In the case of a pull hook, you can't say anything about a swing simply by observing the flight of the ball. As far as the swing is concerned, you've tilted the clubface to the left. You can't determine the path of the swing exactly. The ball might already have started out to the left because you rotated the clubface to the left, even though the path of the swing didn't move from the outside

in. In order to say anything concrete about the path of the swing, you have to look at the divot and, if possible, a video-tape. Another way of analyzing your shots is to look at those that are not pull hooks. These shots might provide informa-tion about whether or not the club approaches the ball from the outside.

The same holds true for the push slice, but in this case, you've tilted the clubface too far to the right. Here, too, you can't make a definite decision about the path of the swing. You'll need to use the same methods outlined above for the pull hook.

A pull slice occurs when the club moves from the outside in and the clubface tilts to the right in relation to the path of the swing.

In the case of a push hook, the path of the swing moves from the inside out, and the face of the club tilts to the left in relation to the path of the swing.

To make corrections your-self, do what a golf teacher would. First, analyze the flight of the ball and try to deter-mine what mistakes you made at the moment of impact. If you are able to determine how you deviated from the optimal swing at the moment of im-pact, you will be able to elimi-nate the faulty technique.

15

Analyzing mistakes is a process of observing what happens "after," in order to understand what went wrong "before." You recognize the mistake by observing the flight of the ball, which comes after the moment of impact.

A perfect divot is uniform in depth, begins slightly to the left of the original position of the ball, and points slightly to the left.

The Divot

When you analyze the moment of impact, the most accurate information comes from reading the divot. When you are using an iron, a perfect divot is one that you hit immediately after the spot where you placed the ball. This is true because, at the moment of impact, the iron is moving downward and pointing slightly to the left and the club is already moving to the inside. The ideal divot has uniform depth since, at the moment of impact, the club is parallel to the ground.

If the divot points too far to the left or right, you can assume that the direction of the swing was moving from the in-

side out or from the outside in, respectively. If the divot is in front of the spot where the ball was, the lowest point of the swing was too far to the right. This occurs when you use a spooning movement or when you swing the club through the ball from the inside out.

If the divot is too deep, the plane of the arm movement was too steep or the angle of approach was too steep. The direction of the swing might be moving from the outside in or, at the moment of impact, too much of your weight was to the left.

If the shot produces no divots at all, the plane of the arm movement was too flat, and, at the moment of impact, the shaft of the club was not in the correct position relative to its lie because your hands were too high on the grip.

Correction Through Exaggeration

Golf instructors often confront the following phenomenon: A student watches a video of his game. After analyzing it, the student understands his mistakes and the effects they have. The student is now ready to correct his mistakes. After a few sessions, he feels that he has acquired a completely new technique. He can't believe it when his instructor informs him that his current swing is almost identical to his previous swing. He wants to know how that can be true. In fact, changing a habitual movement feels so extreme that the student thinks that he has gone to the other extreme when, in reality, he is only carrying out a neutral movement. For example, a player who is moving the club too far to the inside on the backswing (on a plane that is too flat) feels he is pulling the club back down in an extremely steep curve when he must bring the club back to its proper plane.

During practice, golfers usually are too timid in correcting their mistakes. However, if they have the courage to exaggerate, and thus achieve a neutral swing and hit the ball with much greater success, they usually complain that this couldn't possibly be the proper swing because it feels so extreme. The only answer is, "You have to decide whether

ANALYZING MISTAKES

you want to continue feeling comfortable, swinging in your old habitual way, accepting the same poor results, or to make use of this chance to greatly improve your game by accepting some discomfort for a while."

While it is easy to convince a student to improve his swing during a lesson, it is much more difficult to change old habits permanently. And that is why most players return to their old mistakes.

How can these experiences help you improve your game by yourself? When you change habits, you should never rely on how the change feels, because feelings are not objective and always depend on what you have done in the past.

Be bold when trying to correct mistakes, even if that means being uncomfortable. Going to the opposite extreme for a little while is not nearly as tragic as continuing to repeat the same mistake over and over again.

When you reach a point where nothing seems to go right, you'll know that you have fallen back into your old habits.

Fundamentals
....

▶ *In order to make corrections, you must first find where you are deviating from the ideal at the moment of impact. Several faults that occur at the moment of impact can be responsible for different mistakes.*

▶ *In order to find any problems at the moment of impact, carefully observe the flight of the ball. You can determine the factors that are responsible for your mistakes by knowing the laws governing the flight of a ball and by observing the behavior of the ball at the moment of impact and when in flight.*

▶ *When practicing your corrections, always exaggerate.*
....

The principle of exaggeration is particularly effective in correcting the swing.

ANALYZING MISTAKES

MISTAKES IN THE LONG GAME

The better you are at analyzing and correcting your mistakes, the faster you will see results.

Slices

As golfers try to improve their game, they usually go through three phases. Each phase has its typical mistakes. During the first phase, golfers seldom hit the ball properly. Instead, they top balls, produce fat hits, and hit the ball with either the tip or the heel of the clubhead. In overcoming these problems, golfers usually enter a slice phase. In this period, most long hits veer off to the right.

In the third phase, the draw phase, the ball starts out to the right and then veers to the left, towards the target. Only in the third phase can golfers hope to lower their handicaps. In the slice phase, a mistake will cost distance because the ball will fly too high. In this case, the clubface has rotated to the right, considerably increasing the loft of the club. This almost always occurs when golfers use a long iron or a wood.

But the height of the ball is not the only problem that can cost distance. A swing from the outside in, used to compensate for the ball veering to the right, can have the same effect when you don't execute the swing properly. This creates a path in which the club approaches the ball at a steeper angle. The energy behind the swing is not moving in the direction of the target. Instead, it is literally moving into the ground.

However, the steep approach used with a short iron does not hurt shots. For longer

When the clubface opens, the actual loft increases, and the ball flies higher.

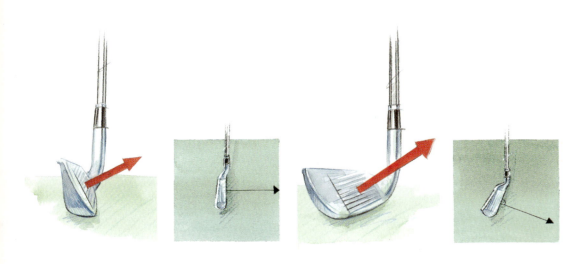

When a club hits through the ball from the outside in, the angle of approach is very steep.

23

shots, the clubface should approach the ball at a much flatter angle so that the energy of the swing moves in the direction of the target. In addition, when you use longer clubs, rotating the clubface will influence a sidespin much more than when using a shorter club, because the speed of the clubhead is greater and the club has less loft. A 9 iron produces only one-eighth of the sidespin a driver produces, assuming identical rotation of the clubface.

All in all, seven factors affect a slice. What follows is a more detailed discussion of those factors.

With a neutral grip, the V created by the hands points to the right collarbone.

Grip

The grip and flexion of the wrists directly influence the position of the clubface at the moment of impact. Therefore, they ought to be checked first.

If you stand in the address position with your arms relaxed, the back of your hands will form an approximate right angle; they are not parallel to each another. You must use this position for your hands in the address position. When you hold a club, your right hand will be a little bit lower than your left hand, and your whole upper body will tilt slightly to the right.

Both hands rotate slightly to the right of the club, and both the Vs created by your thumbs and index fingers point to the collarbone. The great speed of the downswing will return your hands to this position for a few seconds, bringing the clubface straight to the ball. If, however, at the beginning of the swing, your hands are holding the club too far to the left, the automatic return of your hands to the address position during the downswing will rotate the clubface to the right as the club approaches the ball. Make sure, therefore, that your hands are far enough to the right so that both Vs point to your right shoulder.

A slice grip usually causes

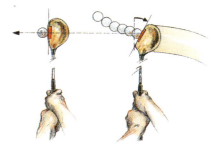

If you rotate your hands too far to the left, the clubface will open during the downswing.

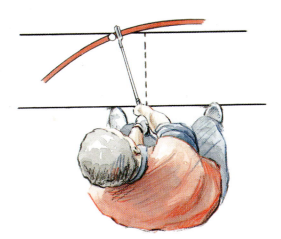

one shoulder to point too far to the left of the target. This creates the same situation as the wrong ball position, in which the ball is too far to the left.

In order to hit a straight ball or a draw, you must move your right shoulder and the ball back a little bit. Another mistake in gripping the club that encourages a slice is a left thumb stretched too far. You have a more difficult time moving your wrists and forearms in this position, and the club doesn't close sufficiently during the downswing.

To find the correct position for your left thumb, grip the club and pull your thumb up as far as possible. Then stretch it down as far as possible. The spot between these two extremes is the proper position.

Gripping a club for a slice usually forces the shoulder too far to the left of the target, leaving the ball too far away from the left foot.

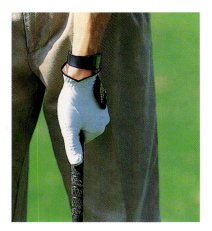

If you stretch your left thumb too far, you have a more difficult time moving your wrists and forearms.

25

In the ideal position, the edge of the clubface and your lower left arm are parallel at the highest point of the backswing (left). . . .

Flexing the Wrists

You can also twist the clubface with the action of your wrists. Ideally, the front edge of the clubface is always parallel to the lower left arm.

If you flex your left wrist towards the back of your hand during the backswing, the clubface will open. To prevent this, make sure that at the end of the backswing your hands are under the club and that your right hand is in position to carry a tray. The back of your left hand and your left forearm will almost be in a straight line.

If both hands are far enough to the right at the beginning of the swing and the right hand is underneath the club at the end of the backswing but the ball is still veer-

. . . If you flex your left wrist towards the back of your hand, the clubface opens and is no longer parallel to the lower left arm (right).

ing off to the right, you are making one of these mistakes in your swing: *classic slice, modern slice, plateau slice, late slice, reverse pivot slice.*

Most golfers have a difficult time figuring out their particular type of slice. In order to make it easier, we have highlighted each of the five types and listed their specific characteristics.

Classic Slice

Characteristics

- *Pull slice starting out flat*
- *Poor half shots and pitches*
- *Divots on extreme left, very deep, and clearly to the left of the ball*
- *Shanks (sockets)*
- *Underhit balls*
- *Problems with balance during swing*

During a neutral swing, your shoulders move on a relatively flat plane, and your arms move upwards on a somewhat steeper plane.

This is not all that simple because different parts of your body must move in different directions. This often leads to mistakes. When your arms and the club move on a flatter plane, they are too close to your body, and the swing is back instead of upwards. When this happens, the same thing usually occurs during the downswing. In other words, your arms are not moving down. Instead, they stay close to the body and follow its rotation. This is the reason that your body comes too far for-ward and the club swings through the ball from a steep angle from the outside in, which you don't want. (However, the steeper the plane of the club, the less your forearm rotates.) The result is that balls that start out to the left veer sharply to the right, creating the pull slice.

In order to solve this problem, your arms must move on

Your hands must move upwards, and your shoulders must rotate on a much flatter plane.

In the case of a classic slice, your club, arms, and body remain too close together. The club swings too far back and then too far forward in the downswing (left).

A close stance almost always prevents you from making exaggerated movements and is very helpful when your problem is a classic slice.

a plane that is steeper than that of your shoulders. Usually most slicers are successful when they temporarily assume a special address position, pulling their right shoulder far back in an extreme fashion. This sets the stage for their shoulders to rotate on a flatter plane, and all they have to concentrate on is swinging their arms high up and back down again.

This address position is also helpful in getting a better feel for the downswing. The goal here is to keep your shoulders slightly to the right, even at the moment of impact. This position will guarantee that the club approaches the ball from the inside instead from the outside.

When you use a proper swing, you must put the ball in a different position. In fact, the more a swing moves from the outside in, the more important it is to position the ball closer to the left foot. In addition to correcting the path of the swing, you must be sure that you are playing the ball more from the center.

A correct stance is one in which your feet are absolutely parallel to each other. During the swing, this stance will give you a sense that your arms and the club must move on different planes so that your body can remain in balance.

During the downswing, the movement of the classic slice forces your body forward towards your toes. This close stance keeps the body still and helps the hands move upward and down again. These two factors can quickly improve your motion and the flight of the ball. Unfortunately, many golfers have doubts about using these ideas on the course. However, if you have a choice between a somewhat unorthodox position that assures good ball movement and your unsuccessful, but standard, position, the decision ought not to be very difficult. The only reason to resume using a normal address position is that you are starting to hit too many push hooks; in other words, if the ball starts out veering to the right instead of to the left.

Use this so-called exercise position only while doing practice swings. Return to your neutral position for the actual swing.

Correcting the classic slice can take time. Even if your attempts do not lead to success within a week and you are still not able to hit the ball straight from a neutral address position, trying corrections is better than doing nothing at all about your slicing.

When you rotate your upper body properly, your shoulders rotate on a flat plane, while your arms swing up and then down.

Modern Slice

Characteristics
- *High push slice*
- *Hitting with tip*
- *Hitting with too much bottom*
- *Good shots with short irons*

A modern slice is exactly the opposite of a classic slice. Here your shoulders follow the steep movement of your arm during the backswing when you pull the club back and it is not open enough. We call such a steep rotation of your shoulders, with the spine moving forward and the head bent down, tilting. The result is almost always a mirrorlike forward movement, with the body tilting again and the club not close enough.

The first cause of this movement might be a position in which your upper body bends too far forward because you have locked your knees. The more your upper body tilts forward, the steeper the plane of your shoulder rotation will be.

In order for your shoulders to rotate on a flatter plane, you must lower your seat without significantly bending your knees and without bending the upper body forward more than 30 degrees.

In order to correct the modern slice, you should practice shots with the ball posi-

In the modern slice, the body tips forward during the backswing, blocking the movement of the downswing (left).

Because the golfer has locked his knees, he bends too far forward. This often causes tilting during the backswing (right).

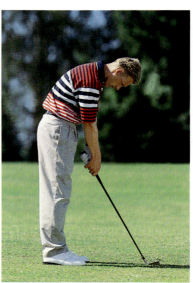

tioned a considerable distance in front of your feet. The result is a round swing similar to a baseball swing. During the backswing, the club opens up, and, during the downswing, it closes up again.

Moving the club on such a plane makes it easy to hit balls with left spin. After a couple of practice shots from this position you should try to hit off the tee from a normal position. Usually, a club moving on the steep swing of a modern slice penetrates the ground too much. However, straightening up slightly during the downswing, pulling the arms up slightly, or creating a spoon-like movement usually provides enough compensation to avoid hitting the ground.

If your backswing is more rounded, habit will lead you to make an unnecessary compensating movement during the downswing. After a few exercises, you will recognize that making yourself taller becomes unnecessary, and this reaction will stop all by itself. In order to reach this point, try hitting a few balls from the tee in a flatter position.

A second reason for the modern slice may be the mistaken belief that, in order to assure a straight shot, the club must move on a straight plane and the clubface must remain straight as long as possible. But that is the mistake. Because the ball is not under your feet but in front of them, the club moves on a circular

In the proper position, you bend your knees just a little so that your upper body is only slightly forward (left).

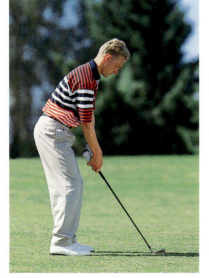

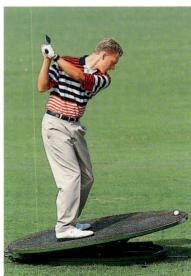

Placing the ball higher than your feet is very helpful in counteracting the modern slice because your swing will become rounder (right).

path, opening during the backswing and closing again during the downswing. This is the only way to bring the clubhead straight to the ball on a regular basis.

If you have difficulty with the proper movement on the course, take a few baseball swings before each shot instead of using your regular practice swing. The feeling created by the baseball swing remains with your body for a couple of seconds. If you then immediately swing at the ball, you will recognize that your swing is much rounder.

Most golfers find it easier to swing the club on a plane that is flatter than their arms. Make sure that by trying to achieve a rounder swing you are not making the backswing flatter, only to lift your arms even higher at the end of the downswing. The result would simply be a change from a modern slice to a classic slice.

Try correcting your backswing so that when the club is parallel to the ground for the first time, it is also parallel to the line to the target. Then, simply move your arms back and closer to your body.

Because the ball is in front of the player, the club must move in a circle. During the swing, the club will open and then close again.

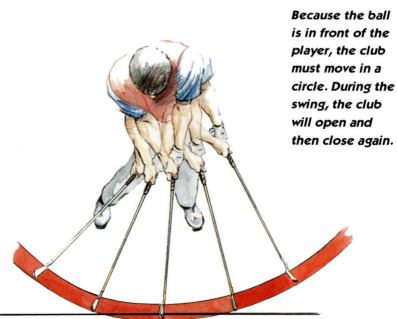

Plateau Slice

Characteristics
- Pull slice starts out flat
- Good half shots and pitches
- Deep divots more pronounced on left, clearly left of ball
- Underhit balls
- Good hits from rough

At the beginning, if the club starts to go to the outside and points too far to the left at the highest point of the backswing, then usually during the downswing the path of the swing tilts to the left. In addition, the club approaches the ball on the steep plane from the outside in. The club is on a steep angle and not closed enough, and the clubface is too open when it approaches the ball.

This slice is easy to correct. Simply place a carton behind the ball in such a way that you cannot move the club outward during the swing. By rotating your shoulders earlier and more forcefully during the backswing, the club will move back so that at the highest point of the backswing it is pointing to the right, past the target. If you move the club out or approach the ball from the outside, the club will hit the carton. This kind of practice is very effective in correcting a plateau slice. If you are having difficulty rotating your shoulders during the backswing because of diminished mobility, try increasing the rotation of your hips. This will create less muscle tension. However, those who are able to completely rotate their shoulders and to keep the rotation of the hips down should most certainly do so. The left foot then remains on the ground and increases the speed of the clubhead.

Here, too, you should first practice from a tee in order to hit the ball cleanly, in spite of the flatter angle at the moment of impact. Then, when you play from the grass, make sure that you do not play the ball too much off your left foot because that does not fit the changed movement.

By the way, you can use the plateau slice to your advantage if you want to play the ball to fade deliberately. Place the ball closer to your left foot and tilt the whole path of the swing towards the left. The ball will then start out to the left and rotate to the right.

With a plateau slice, the
whole plane of the swing
tilts to the left. The club
starts out to the outside
and approaches the ball
from the outside.

Late Slice

Many golfers believe that you only play with the left side of your body. In addition, photos of top golfers taken from the front show that their club and their left arm form an extreme angle shortly before the moment of impact. Thus, many players conclude that they can increase the length of a shot by pulling with their left hand. However, they forget that top players usually fight against a hook.

Another common misconception is that you can counteract a slice, supposedly created by the exaggerated use of your right shoulder, by increasing the rotation of your hips during the downswing. Here, too, the result might be a late hit and an even more pronounced slice.

Since the concept of how to swing a golf club influences your swing, you should understand that dealing with a slice this way only increases it. In fact, the later the angle between your left arm and shoulder dissolves, the more difficult it becomes to bring your hands and the clubhead to the ball at the same moment.

If, however, at the moment of impact your hands are too far ahead of the ball, the clubhead is usually open. The reason for a late slice, therefore, might lie in a grip that is too high. You cannot hold on tight to the club and at the same time keep your wrists loose. However, this is necessary so that the angle created between your left arm and the club dur-

Whenever the angle between your left arm and the club dissolves too late, the clubface is open when it approaches the ball.

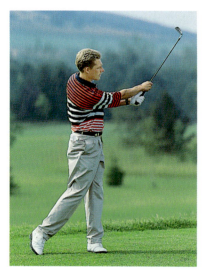

When using this temporary grip, the angle between your left arm and the club will open faster.

ing the backswing opens up again during the downswing.

Using a different grip is a good exercise to eliminate late hits. Simply move your lower hand a little bit farther down, preferably as far as the end of the grip.

Use this type of grip in the beginning only when you practice from the tee, since the hit will feel rather unusual. Because of the lower position of the right hand, the angle between your arm and the club will dissolve earlier, and the clubface will open earlier.

However, make sure that an earlier hit does not turn into a wrong hit in which your left wrist flexes towards the back of your hand. This creates a spooning movement which leads to fat hits and high balls. This exercise makes it possible for almost every player to hit balls that veer off to the left. After you have achieved this on a regular basis, slowly work yourself back to a normal grip by moving your right hand little by little back towards your left hand.

Reverse Pivot Slice

Characteristics
- *Slices start out flat*
- *Deep divots*
- *Underhit balls*
- *Problems maintaining balance during the swing*

Another reason why balls seem to regularly veer off to the right is that you have not distributed your weight properly. During the backswing, if your upper body does not rotate around the spinal column to

In a reverse pivot slice, your upper body does not move far enough behind the ball and instead moves ahead of the club during the downswing.

Hits from a higher position help to counter-act a reverse pivot slice. It's easier keeping your body be-hind the ball.

the right but rather shifts to the left in the direction of the target, your weight is too far to the left of the ball.

During the downswing, if your body usually moves to the left of the intended line to the target because of the momen-tum of the club, your body will also be too far to the left at the moment of impact.

During the back-swing, proper rotation of the body results in your head moving one-half its width to the right.

The club is unable to catch up with the body during the swing and, therefore, doesn't close enough at the moment of impact.

A reverse pivot slice usually occurs when you try to keep your head in the same position during the swing while trying to rotate around the axis running through the center of your body. This leads to an improper distribution of your weight.

In order to make the proper corrections, practice on an inclined plane. Standing on an incline allows gravity to pull your body to the right, preventing your body from falling back to the left during the downswing. In such a position, every ball always veer to the left. The correct movement during the backswing allows your spine to remain in place, permitting your head to move to the right only the distance of one width of the head.

Even if in the beginning you feel that you are moving too far away from the ball during the backswing, be consistent. This is the only way to stay farther behind the ball at the moment of impact, allowing the club to stay with the movement of the body.

Reasons for Slices

....

▶ *Hands too far to the left on the grip; ball and shoulder too far forward.*
▶ *Left wrist flexed to the back of your hand during the backswing.*
▶ *Arms remain too close to the body, backswing and downswing take place on two entirely different planes, and club approaches ball on a steep angle (classic slice).*
▶ *Club opens too little during the backswing, and the body tips; in downswing, club isn't closed enough and body is blocked (modern slice).*
▶ *Path of swing tilts to the left; because of insufficient body rotation, club starts to the outside and moves into the ball from the outside (plateau slice).*
▶ *Angle between your left arm and club opens up too late; hands at the moment of impact are too far ahead of ball, and clubface is open (late slice).*
▶ *Due to lack of side movement during backswing, body is too far to the left and clubface is open at moment of impact (reverse pivot slice).*

....

Hooks

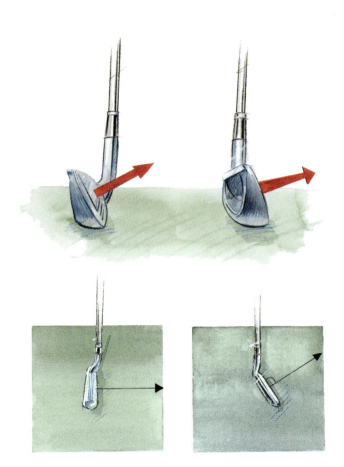

In addition to balls veering off to the left, another problem with hooking is that the club approaches the ball on a plane that is too flat because the path of the swing usually comes from the inside out. This makes hitting out of the rough and hitting off bare ground very difficult.

In addition, a closed clubface reduces the loft of the club, making it difficult to get the ball airborne with a long iron or a driver. As is the case with the slice, the problem with hooking lies in the fact that the clubface tilts. Here, too, you need to check your grip and wrist flexion, the two most important factors influencing the position of the clubface.

When you close the clubface, you reduce the actual loft, and the flight path of the ball is flat.

If the club moves through the ball from the inside out, the approach to the ball is too flat.

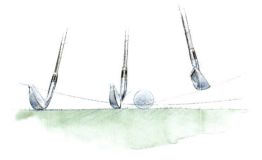

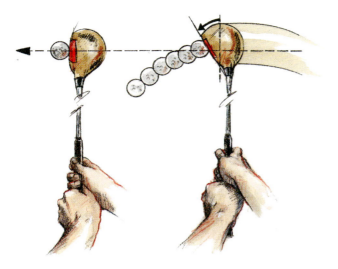

If your rotate your hands on the grip too far to the right, the clubface will close during the downswing.

The Grip

At the beginning of the swing, if you rotate your hands too far to the right on the grip, when your hands return to their natural position during the downswing, they will cause the clubface to rotate to the left at the moment of impact.

Be sure, therefore, that your hands are far enough to the left so that both Vs point to your chin. A hook grip usually causes your shoulder to point too far to the right of the target and the ball to be too far to the right. In order to hit a straight hit, however, your right shoulder and the ball must be farther forward.

A hook grip usually causes your shoulder to point too far to the right of the target. You then play the ball too far from your right foot.

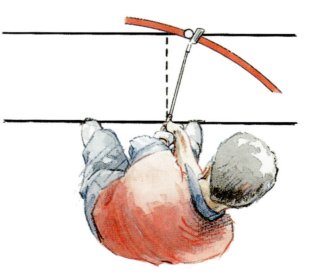

Flexing the Wrist

Flexing your wrists improperly can also cause hooks. Ideally, the front edge of the clubface is always parallel to your left lower arm.

If you bend your left wrist towards your palm during the backswing, the clubface will close. The wrong grip is the culprit here. If you are not holding the club properly in your left hand, your left wrist usually bends in the direction of the back of your hand. Then you are not gripping the club with the pads of your hand and thumb but too far back in the palm of your hand instead of your fingers.

In this case, make sure you hold the club with your fingers and the left pad of your hand. Place the club between the pad of your hand and your index finger.

This grip guarantees that you will hold the club properly. All you need to do then is close the rest of the fingers. If you are using the proper grip and your wrists still flex in the wrong direction in the first part of the swing, try to guide the club back with more forearm rotation while simultaneously bending your wrists. This will force the club to move in the right plane, and your left wrist will bend in the proper direction.

If your left wrist bends towards the palm of your hand, the club-face closes and is not parallel to the lower left arm.

If you grip the club in a steep angle with your left hand, your wrist often bends towards the palm of your hand.

43

THE LONG GAME

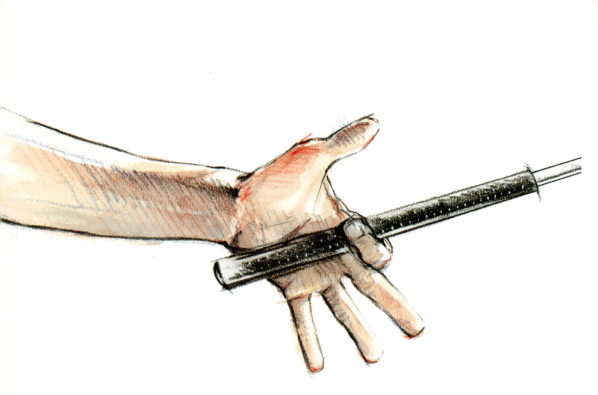

If you let the club cross the palm of your hand on a diagonal from the pad to your index finger, you are holding it correctly.

If your grip and the position of your wrists are correct, the clubface is open again at the highest point of the backswing. The ball may still be veering to the right. Three things could happen during the swing, and we will discuss them now.

Flat Hook

Characteristics
- Balls are flying too low
- Thin hits
- Topped balls
- Shanks (sockets)
- Good tee woods
- Bad hits with short irons

If your arms move on a plane that is too flat during the backswing, your forearm rotation will be too strong during the downswing.

You can easily demonstrate this to yourself by doing a few baseball swings with your golf club. When your forearm rotation is too severe, the club closes too early and tilts to the left at the moment of impact.

You can remedy this problem by doing a few practice swings on a down slope where the ball is lower than your feet. This position will force you to swing the club on a steeper plane so that your arms and the club move farther in front of your body, and the clubface will not close as quickly during the downswing.

In the beginning, practicing on a down slope is extremely difficult for those golfers whose swing plane is too flat.

Therefore, in the beginning, practice with a short iron and do half swings. Don't try to force the club down by bending down during the downswing. You should hit the divot solely by moving the club and the arms on a steeper plane.

The angle of the path is too exaggerated when your clubhead crosses the intended line to the target from the outside after the moment of impact. In this case, the plane of your arm movement is probably still too flat, and you should practice what we have suggested here.

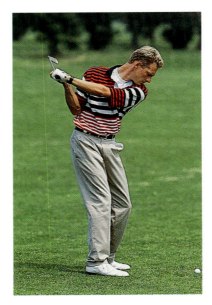

If your arms move on a plane that is too flat, you create too much forearm rotation, and the club closes too early.

45

A ball placed lower than your feet creates a steeper path and less hook.

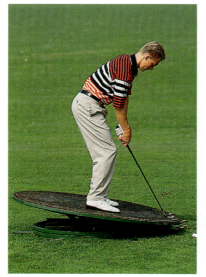

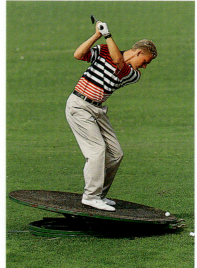

Spooned Hook

When the club-head is ahead of your hands during the downswing, it usually reaches the ball in a closed position, creating a hook.

If the clubhead is ahead of the hands during the downswing, it is usually in a closed position when it reaches the ball, and the ball veers off to the left. This problem is almost always the result of too little hip rotation during the downswing.

During the downswing, if your hips don't move out of the way but remain in place, the hands usually keep on moving independently. The result is a closed clubface. In order to solve this problem, concentrate on moving your hips slightly to the left during the downswing and on keeping your hands in front of the ball at the moment of impact. This will free the club a little later.

Correcting your downswing is always difficult because the movement only takes one-fifth of a second. Try the following exercises. Start swinging the club back as you usually do, and then try to do only the first part of the downswing twice. On the third attempt, hit the ball without going into the address position. This is often the only exercise that can really change your downswing technique.

So your hands are in front of the ball at the moment of impact, move your hips to the side, out of the way.

47

In the plateau
hook, the swing
plane rotates
completely to
the right. The
club starts out
too far inside
and approaches
from inside the
ball.

Plateau Hook

Characteristics
- *Gaining height immediately*
- *Bad half shots, pitches, and short irons*
- *Divots pointing to right or entirely missing when using an iron*
- *Fat hits*
- *Good woods*
- *Problems hitting out of rough and from bare ground*

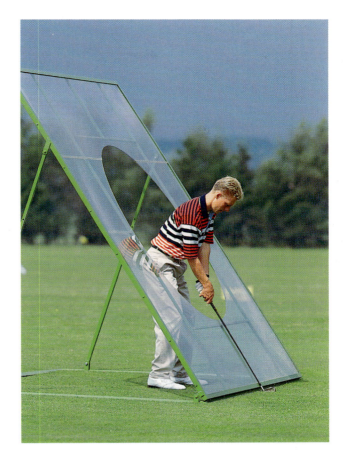

If you pull a club back too far during the backswing and at the highest point of the swing the club points to the right, the club will obviously move to the right during the downswing. The club will hit the ball too far from the inside and on an angle that is too flat.

To correct this hook, do a few practice hits with a swing stand. This type of training equipment makes it impossible to pull the club back too flat.

In the beginning, practicing with this equipment will be irritating because you will be convinced that the club is moving back without shoulder rotation. However, golfers who suffer from plateau hooks usually rotate their shoulders too much. If this training equipment is not available to you, use a carton and place it in the appropriate location on the ground. Since you may have a difficult time getting a feeling for what direction the clubhead is pointing, concentrate more on the grip. Insert a tee in the end of the grip. When you take the club back on the correct plane, the tee

When you practice with a swing plane, you cannot move the club back on a low plane, so the club won't approach the ball on a too-flat angle.

49

After making a correction, insert a tee into the end of the grip. Viewed from your perspective, it should point to the right and forward rather than behind you.

Reasons for Hooking

▶ *Hands rotated too far to the right.*
▶ *Left wrist bent towards the palm of the hand during backswing.*
▶ *Arms and club move on a plane that is too flat, causing too much lower arm rotation which closes the clubface too early (flat hook).*
▶ *Clubhead ahead of hands during downswing, causing the clubface to point towards the right (spooned hook) at the moment of impact.*
▶ *Plane of swing tilted towards the right; club moving too far to the inside and approaching the ball on a plane that is too flat (plateau hook).*

should point to the line to the target.

When you make this correction, your arms must move primarily in front of your body rather than behind your body. The farther your hands move behind your body, the farther the clubhead will be in front of your body. Thus, you must frequently adjust the placement of the ball, always checking that you don't place it too far to the right.

Topping and Thin Hits

You can frequently see topped hits by watching beginners. These hits are very discouraging since a topped ball usually rolls along the ground, never going very far. You top the ball when you are too busy looking where the ball is going before you even hit the ball. You raise your body, taking the club with you, hitting only the top of the ball. In order to correct this mistake, you must keep your head down as long as possible during the follow-through so that you don't follow the movement of the ball too early. But this correction creates two more problems:
1. An expansive follow-through, in which you cannot swing the club through the ball in a downward motion.
2. You put a great deal of stress on your spine because you hollow your back in order to keep your head in a low position as you rotate towards the target.

Because you're afraid to lift your head too early, you lower it too much in the address position. This causes your whole upper body to bend too far forward. This position creates a great deal of painful stress on the back.

Logic tells us that a player will try to prevent such pain by trying to right himself. In that sense, any attempt to exaggerate the correct stance by bending the upper body forward has the exact opposite effect. Instead, observe the flight of the ball with your head raised, this makes it much easier to

When the club approaches the ball from the inside, the clubhead hits the ball on the upswing; so it hits too high.

51

rotate your shoulders properly without surrendering the upright position.

Pulling your left arm up doesn't cause the clubhead to hit the ball above its equator. This is never the reason for topping. Therefore, the left arm doesn't need to remain rigid during the swing. Actually, if you keep your left arm unnaturally straight in the address position or during the backswing, you'll need to pull it in more during the downswing in order to prevent being injured when your club hits the ground at the wrong angle.

This is less likely to happen if you bend your arms slightly during the backswing since the centrifugal energy of your movement stretches your arms out anyway during the downswing. If you pull your arm in during the downswing and follow-through, you are compensating for allowing the club to approach the ball on a plane

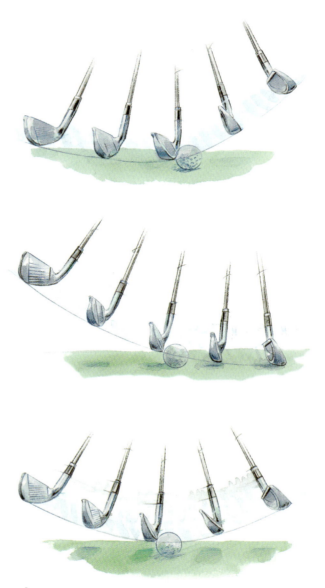

You can top a ball during the upward movement of the follow-through (top), in the downward movement (middle), or at the lowest point of the follow-through (below). In each case, the point of impact is too high.

that is too steep. This is the case when the club swings from the outside in.

Three problems are responsible for topping:

1. The deepest point of the follow-through is too far to the right, and the clubhead is moving upwards instead of down at the moment of impact (topping from the inside or a spooned top).
2. The lowest point of the follow-through is too far to the left, and the clubhead is too high at the moment of impact (topping from the outside or late topping).
3. The lowest point of the follow-through is too high, and the club is not low enough throughout the swing (flat topping).

Topping from the Inside

Characteristics
- Topped shots that move to the right, particularly half shots and pitches
- Hooks or pushed balls
- Divots that lean to the right or are absent when using an iron
- Fat hits
- Good woods
- Problems hitting out of rough or from bare spots

At the moment of impact, if the clubhead is moving to the right—in other words, through the ball from the inside out—the lowest point of the swing will automatically be

Bending your head down too far makes it impossible for you to hit downwards and to have a proper follow-through.

to the right, and the club will move upwards too early.

For that reason, many divots point to the right, and the ball often takes off to the right, regardless of whether or not you topped it. To solve this problem, you have to move the club more in front of your body during the backswing and the downswing. At the highest point of the backswing, allow the shaft of the club to point more to the right and try to hit a divot to the left of the ball.

Another good exercise for correcting topping from the inside is to play off a tee placed in front of your left foot. If you swing the club too much from the inside out, you'll miss the ball entirely.

The goal of this exercise is to hit the ball straight to the left, in spite of the tee, creating a divot after you have hit the ball.

Another reason the club approaches the ball too much from the inside is an inefficient body rotation during the downswing. At the moment of impact, if your arms swing down while your shoulders and hips are still too far to the right, the club reaches the lowest point of the swing before hitting the ball. In this case, it makes sense to increase the rotation of your lower body because that rotation pulls your upper body with it. In that sense, it provides a bet-

During exercises, if you hit a ball positioned far from your left foot, the club is less likely to move through the ball from the inside.

ter path for the club to follow. However, if you have sufficient body rotation and the club still approaches the ball too much from the inside, don't increase your rotation. While this would bring the club swing into a better plane, the club would still be too far behind, relative to the body. In this case, you have to bring the club farther in front by increasing your forearm rotation.

If the clubhead is ahead of your hands before the moment of impact, it will move upwards after the moment of impact.

Spooned Topping

Characteristics
- *High balls*
- *Fat hits with divots pointing straight to target*
- *Hitting with tip of clubhead*
- *Hooks*
- *Problems hitting out of the rough*
- *Problems hitting from bare spots*

The club can also hit the ball during the upward movement of the follow-through. This occurs because, at the moment of impact, your hands are ahead of the club, even though the club is moving in the right direction. In other words, you spoon the ball. In this case, the follow-through feels tight. Whenever your hands are behind the ball at the moment of impact, you increase the loft and well-hit balls fly too high and sometimes hook. To solve this problem, practice only half shots in the beginning. Stop immediately after the moment of impact to check if your left arm is extended and in a straight line with the club shaft.

If the clubhead passes your hands before the moment of impact, the club shaft will be an extension of your right arm. During the correction, make sure that you are not simply delaying the shot.

Often golfers don't correct

THE LONG GAME

a spooned topping properly because they believe it is an early hit. However, if your left wrist bends towards the back of your hand immediately before the moment of impact, the shot is not an early hit but an incorrect one. Therefore, simply delaying the hit is wrong because that only leads to a slice. At the moment of impact, your hands need to be ahead of the ball. At the same time, however, the clubface must face the ball straight on. For that to happen, your left wrist must flex towards the palm of your hand.

If you carry out the correction properly, the club hits the ball first, then hits the divot. In order to hit a correct shot with an iron, you must hit a divot. While a hit without a divot may turn out to be a success, it will never lead to consistency.

The proper release is not something that a player can learn in five minutes. Take slow swings more often and move your left wrist now and then without a club just as it should be at the moment of

In order for the club to move through the ball during the downward movement, you must flex your left wrist in the direction of the palm of your hand.

impact: your left lower arm rotates counterclockwise, and your wrist angles to the side of your small finger, bent in the direction of the palm of your hand.

Topping from the Outside

Characteristics
- *Topped balls start to left with longer clubs*
- *Pulls and slices with longer clubs*
- *Deep divots pointing to extreme left, hit very deep, and clearly hit to left of ball*
- *Shanks (sockets)*
- *Underhit balls*

The second reason for topping a ball is that the club is too far to the left of the ball immediately before the moment of impact.

If the club is moving towards the left at the moment of impact—in other words, swinging through the ball from the outside in—the vertex of the swing will shift too much before it reaches the ball, and the club will hit the ball too high. For that reason, topped balls usually start towards the left. Those that

If the club approaches the ball from the outside, the clubhead usually hits the ball above the equator.

57

In order for the
club to approach
the ball more
from the inside,
it should point
slightly to the
left of the target
at the highest
point of the
backswing.

you don't top are usually either sliced or pulled. In order to correct this error, the club has to approach the ball more from the inside. When practicing, make sure that the shaft of the club points directly towards or slightly to the right of the target at the highest point of the backswing. You'll need to use a complete shoulder rotation. During the downswing, move your arms with only slight downward shoulder and hip rotations. By the way, this type of correction is similar to that for the classic slice and for the plateau slice (see page 28 for the exercise).

Late Topping

Characteristics
- *Flat hits*
- *Shanks (sockets)*
- *Pulling the club back with the left arm during the downswing*
- *Slices*

The second reason you hit the ball above the equator is that the angle created between your left arm and the shaft of the club during the backswing dissolves too late during the downswing. Thus, the club

If you dissolve the angle between your left arm and the club too late (late hit), the head of the club will hit the ball above its equator.

hasn't reached the lowest point in the swing when you hit the ball.

This type of late hit occurs because you have not reestablished the original circle at the moment of impact. In order to correct this situation, you must use your wrists earlier in the downswing, creating the feeling that the club must speed up earlier rather than later for it to hit the ground before it reaches the ball.

Since it isn't easy to correct your downswing, try to practice the start of the downswing twice in a row before hitting the ball. In the beginning, practice from a tee. But here, too, make sure that you are not spooning with an earlier hit. While you need to dissolve the angle between your left wrist and lower arm earlier, your left wrist should not flex towards the back of your hand.

At the moment of impact, your left arm and the club shaft should create a straight line.

Flat Topping

Characteristics
- *Tops start out straight*
- *Hooks*
- *Shanks (sockets)*
- *Good tee woods*
- *Bad hits with short irons*

One last possible cause for topping occurs when the lowest point of the curve of your swing is too high. The reason is almost always that the plane of your swing is too flat, which is only appropriate if you want to hit a ball in the air, as you would a baseball. If, however, you want to hit the ball off the ground but not up in the air, your arms and the club must move on a specific plane. In order to get a feeling for what is necessary to bring your arms and club upwards in the backswing, practice hitting with the ball in a position that is lower than your feet.

Another reason the club moves on a plane that is too flat involves the way you hold the club, with both hands rotated too far to the right. This often causes your shoulders to point to the right of the target. Together, these factors can be responsible for your club being on a plane that is too flat.

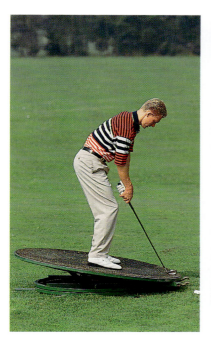

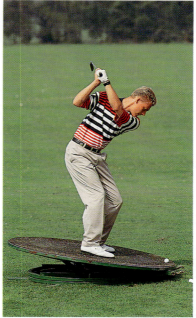

Avoid flat topping by increasing the plane of the swing. It's helpful to position the ball so that it is lower than your feet.

Make sure that you rotate your shoulders at right angles to the spin, or you will bring your body upright. You can also cause flat topping when you bend your knees too much in the address position. This position puts your upper body in a very upright position, forcing you to reach downwards with your arms. When someone observes you from the side, you look as if your arms and the club are in a straight line.

This position makes it almost impossible to avoid a flat swing.

Make sure, therefore, that you make yourself smaller by

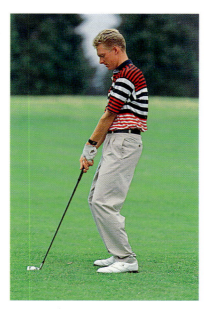

If you bend your knees too much, your upper body tends to be upright, resulting in a flat swing.

61

THE LONG GAME

lowering your seat, bending your upper body in such a way that all you have to do is let your arms hang down.

Reasons for Topping

....

▶ The club approaches the ball too much from the inside. The circle of the swing is at its deepest point before the moment of impact and is already moving upwards when the club hits the ball (topping from the inside).

▶ The clubhead is ahead of your hands during the downswing. The deepest point of the swing occurs before the moment of impact, and the club is swinging upwards again when it reaches the ball (spooned topping).

▶ The club approaches the ball from the outside, and the club has not reached the deepest point in the circle of the swing at the moment of impact, causing the club to swing through the ball too high (topping from the outside).

▶ At the moment of impact, you have not dissolved the angle between your left arm and the club sufficiently, and the club hits the ball above its equator (late topping).

▶ Your arms and the club move in a flat plane. During the backswing, the club and your arms don't move far enough, preventing them from being low enough during the downswing (flat topping).

....

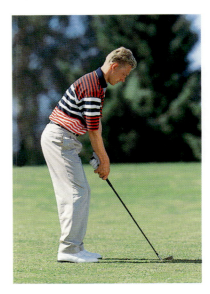

The proper position is knees slightly bent and upper body leaning forward enough for your arms to hang down freely.

Fat Hits

When a clubhead hits the ground before hitting the ball, the result is a fat hit, which always causes a considerable loss of distance because hitting the ground substantially breaks the momentum of the club. If you are not playing the ball far enough from your left foot, you could be making two different types of mistake during the swing. These are fairly simple to correct.

Fat Hits from the Inside

Characteristics
- Divots pointing to right
- Hooks and pushes
- Topped balls that veer to right
- Good woods and bad irons

If the club moves through the ball from the inside out, the deepest point of the swing shifts to the right so that the club usually hits the ground before reaching the ball. As is the case with a topped ball from the inside, here, too, you must move the club more in front of the body so that the

club is on a steeper angle when reaching the ball. At the highest point of the backswing, the club shaft should point more to the left.

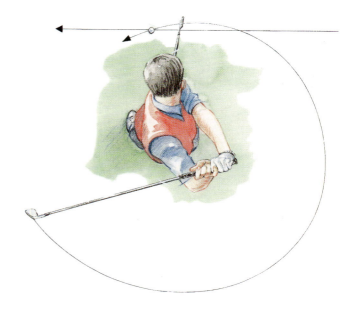

When the club approaches the ball too much from the inside, you must point it more to the left of the target at the highest point of the backswing.

63

Spooned Fat Hits

Characteristics
- *Divots pointing towards target*
- *High balls*
- *Hits made with tip of club*
- *Pull hooks*

If, at the moment of impact, the club is ahead of your hands, the deepest point of the swing also shifts too much to the right, even if your head is moving in the right direction. The exercises in the section on

Reasons for Fat Hits

....

▶ *The ball is too close to your left foot.*
▶ *The direction of the swing is too far from the inside out, and the deepest point of the circle of the swing shifts to the right.*
▶ *The clubhead is ahead of your hands at the moment of impact, and the deepest point of the circle of the swing is to the right.*
▶ *At the moment of impact, your body is too far behind the ball.*

....

topping are helpful. During practice, stop the movement of the club immediately before the moment of impact and check that the shaft of the club forms a continuous straight line with your left arm. This is how you learn how to hit down correctly.

During the backswing, make sure that the lower half of your body doesn't rotate too far to the right. In the down-swing, your body should shift far enough to the left, because if it stays behind too long—in other words to the right—your hands may get in front of the ball.

Fat-hit golfers tend to feel that a hit with a divot is a bad hit because the divot is always in front of the ball. Their instinctive conclusion is to prevent the divot, but this is wrong. Instead, by directing the swing, you must hit the divot farther to the left, by allowing your hands to be in front of the ball at the moment of impact, or by using your body more efficiently.

A spooning
motion always
creates a divot
that is too far
to the right. To
prevent this,
practice half
shots, stopping
your swing as
shown.

65

THE LONG GAME

Hitting with the Heel (Shank)

If you hit a ball at a point closer to the heel instead of with the sweet spot, the club rotates (closes) in your hands. Together with the wrong spot of impact, this leads to a loss of drive, considerably reducing the distance a ball will fly.

If the ball is hit with the hosel or socket, we call the hit a shank, or socket. Here, the ball starts out almost at a right angle. In exceptional cases, especially when using a wood, the ball can veer off to the left.

Sockets, also called shanks, have a simple technical explanation, and it's not as difficult to correct them as you might think. In no case is a socket the result of a psychological problem, as many people assume.

If you hit the ball with the heel of the clubhead, the club will rotate to the left, and the ball will travel only a short distance.

Flat Shank (Socket)

Characteristics
- *Hooks*
- *Thin, topped, and fat hits*
- *Good tee woods*
- *Bad hits with short irons*

The most common reason for these shanks is that the plane of your arms and/or the club is too flat. If your arm and the club move back too far and not high enough during the back-swing, they will move too far forward and not far enough down during the downswing. The result is that the ball is hit with the heel of the club.

Viewed from the side, a club always needs to move a certain distance back as well as a certain distance up. In comparison, however, the movement back is much shorter than the movement upwards.

In order to change this, you must bring the club into the air by bending your wrists instead of using too much lower arm rotation towards the back. Here, too, you'll find it helpful to use a swing plane when practicing.

Your arm movements should not follow your body rotation too much. Instead, during the second phase of the

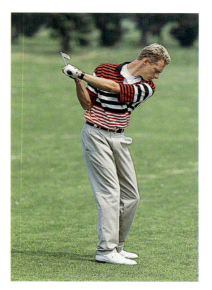

If the arms move too far back during the back-swing, they will come too far forward in the downswing.

During the back-swing, the end of the grip should move upward more, rather than back.

THE **LONG** GAME

Using a swing plane is helpful if you are swinging your arms and the club back too far.

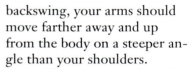

backswing, your arms should move farther away and up from the body on a steeper angle than your shoulders.

You'll want to practice with the ball placed lower than your feet. This will move the swing along a steeper angle. For a proper swing, you must pull the club back solely to the right. You move the club back by simply rotating your shoulders.

Here, the arms are moving at a steeper angle than the shoulders.

Late Shank (Socket)

Characteristics
- Push slice
- Thin, topped, flat hits
- Pulling the club back with the left arm during the downswing

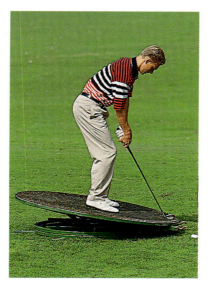

The second reason for a shank is a late hit. If the angle created between your left arm and the club dissolves too late during the downswing, the clubface is unable to close and remains behind too long. The heel of the clubhead reaches the ball way before its tip. Another reason could be that you are holding the grip too tightly or that you are using your left hand to pull the club down. Don't hit the ball as if you were using the edge of your hand. That is wrong. Instead, imagine that you are using the back of your hand. If that were the case, your lower left arm would rotate counterclockwise, and your wrists would straighten out.

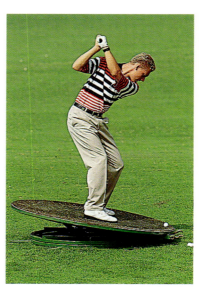

Hitting balls that are lower than your feet will increase the angle of the swing. This prevents you from hitting the ball with the heel.

Classic Slice Shank (Socket)

Characteristics
- *Pull slice starting out flat*
- *Pulls hit with short clubs*
- *Leaving very deep divots pointing way to the left and are clearly to the left of the ball*
- *Underhit balls*
- *Problems with balance during swing*

Another reason for hitting the ball with the heel of the club-head might be that long balls are pull slices. They start out to the left, but in the course of the flight they veer to the right. Here, the club and your arms are usually too far in front because of an open club-face during the downswing.

If your ball consistently veers to the right, you'll soon begin to swing more to the left. The ball then might start out going more to the left, and the slice doesn't look quite so bad. However, in order to swing through the ball to the left—in other words from outside-in—the club has to be too far in front during the downswing. Usually the result is that you hit the ball with the heel of the clubhead. This is especially true when you are using a wood because the ball veers off much more.

In order to remove this source of trouble, you must first make sure that the club-face is not open at the moment of impact. In other words, the clubface is towards the right when it approaches the ball. You can usually find the reason in a faulty grip or in the way you are using your wrists (see the chapter on the slice). As soon as the clubface hits the ball in such a way that it can-not veer off to the right, you have started to initiate the downswing with the club approaching the ball from the inside. In addition, you should concentrate on moving your arms down instead of forward without a lot of shoulder or hip rotation. Then you'll hit the ball with the sweet spot, and your shots will gain con-siderable distance.

Shanks (Sockets) Due to Insufficient Rotation

Characteristics
- *Pull slice*
- *Insufficient distance for long shots*
- *Topped balls*

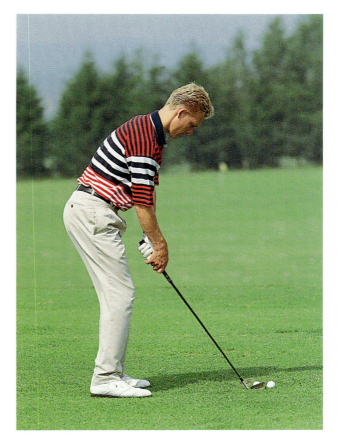

During the backswing, if your shoulders don't rotate enough in relation to the movement of your arms, your shoulder rotation is insufficient during the downswing and moves ahead of your arms. The result is that the club remains open far too long and is too far ahead.

To correct this, you must either shorten your arm swing or increase the rotation of your shoulders. Which of the two is the right one depends on how far your club swings. If you use a full swing and a long club that does not reach the horizontal—in other words covers less than 270 degrees—you need to increase the rotation of your shoulders. If, however, the club moves past 270 degrees, your swing is probably too long. You need to reduce your swing so that at the highest point of the backswing your arms are at the side of your head and not behind. However, do not shorten the whole movement, or the rela-tionship between your shoulder rotation and your arm swing will not improve. Your shoulder rotation needs to be as pronounced as it was before.

After you've made the proper adjustments, try placing a second ball in front of the ball you intend to hit.

The two balls should be approximately the width of a ball apart from each other. After you make the necessary corrections, you usually eliminate

The ultimate test: A second ball placed just above the ball you intend to hit will tell you, if it moves or not, whether you hit with the heel of the club.

If your shoulder does not rotate enough in relation to your arm swing, you hit with the heel of the club.

shanks, but your tendency to hit with the heel remains. A second ball will immediately tell you how successful your corrective measures really were. If the club is just a little bit ahead, you'll also hit the second ball, and it, too, will fly into the air. In that case, you need to practice until the second ball routinely remains in place.

Reasons for Hitting with the Heel

▶ *During the backswing, the club and/or your arms are too flat. In other words, it or they are moving too far back, and during the downswing the club and/or your arms are not far enough in front (flat shank).*

▶ *The angle between your left arm and the club dissolves too late. The open clubface causes the heel of the clubhead to reach the ball before the tip (late shank).*

▶ *During the downswing, the movement of the classic slice allows your arms and the club to reach too far out front, while during the whole swing your arms remain too close to your body (classic slice shank).*

▶ *If the rotation of your shoulders is insufficient in relation to the swing of your arms, then your body rotates ahead of the movement of your arms during the downswing. The result is that your hands and the club-head are on the outside.*

73

Hitting with the Tip

If instead of hitting the ball with the sweet spot you hit it with the tip of the clubhead, the club rotates in your hands (open) and the energy wasted during the process shortens the distance the ball travels.

Hitting the ball with the tip of the clubhead occurs for one of two reasons: a steep swinging angle or a closed clubface. You can determine which of the two is the cause by observing balls that you hit for distance but which you have not hit with the tip. Did you slice them? If so, flatten the plane of your arm movement.

If you hit the ball with the tip of the clubhead, the club rotates to the right and the ball will not fly very far.

Did you hook them? Try moving your hips out of the way quicker during the downswing and delaying the hit.

Swinging on a Steep Plane

Characteristics
- *Insufficient distance*
- *High push slices*
- *Divots too deep*
- *Good hits with short irons*

During the backswing, if your arms and the club move on a steep angle and don't move far enough back, then during the downswing they will also be too steep and not far enough in front. The result is a ball hit with the tip.

In order to flatten the angle of your arms and the club, you can try one of two exercises. The first is to do some baseball swings. These will automatically increase the rotation of your lower arms, moving the club onto a flatter plane as well as allowing your arms to swing farther around your body and to move on a flatter plane. The second exercise in-

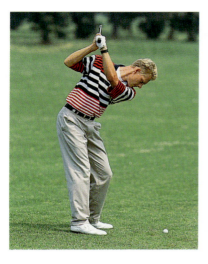

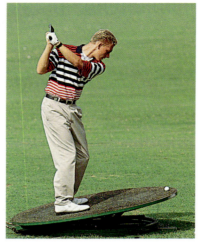

If your arms don't move far enough back during the back-swing, they won't move far enough forward during the downswing. The result is that you hit the ball with the tip (left). Placing the ball higher than your feet is helpful in rounding your swing (right).

volves placing the ball higher than your feet. This also forces your arms and the club into a flatter curve.

Closed Clubface

Characteristics
- *Measurable loss of distance*
- *Hooks*
- *Hits too flat*
- *Hits that are fat or thin*

The second reason for hitting the ball with the tip is that the clubface is too closed. The more closed it is, the more likely that the tip of the club-head will hit the ball first. If

this is the case, make sure that you rotate your hips quickly during the downswing and that they are far enough out of the way; otherwise the club-head moves ahead of the hands too soon, closing the clubface too early.

A good test to see if your correction has been successful is to place one ball behind the one that you want to hit.

Often the changes are so small that you have a difficult time determining if a correction has actually made any difference. If you really want to be sure that the club has hit the ball with the sweet spot, the second ball will tell the story. If the club has moved forward even slightly, you'll also hit the second ball.

Reasons for Hitting with the Tip

....

▶ *During the backswing, the club and/or your arms do not move far enough back and, in turn, not far enough forward. In other words, the plane of the swing is too steep.*
▶ *During the downswing, your hips do not move out of the way quickly enough. The clubhead moves ahead of your hands, and the clubface approaches the ball in a closed position, causing the tip of the clubhead to be ahead of the heel.*

....

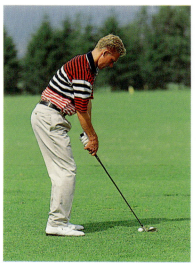

The ultimate test: A second ball just below your target ball will tell you if you hit with the sweet spot, not the tip.

Insufficient Distance

Before you do any of the following exercises designed to increase the speed of your clubhead, make sure that your lack of distance is actually due to the lack of speed of your clubhead and not some mistake at the moment of impact. For instance, if your clubface is always open at the moment of impact, or if you never hit the ball with the sweet spot, or if the club is not at the proper angle when it approaches the ball, you can never achieve great distance. In all these cases you would be wasting your time concentrating on increasing the speed of the clubhead. First, you have to correct your hitting technique. If, however, you fundamentally hit the ball properly, and you still cannot get sufficient distances out of your shots, either you don't use your wrists properly or you are not using your body's tension correctly.

Insufficient Use of the Wrists

Characteristics
- Bad pitches
- Cramped hands
- Exaggerated use of body

If you hit a ball cleanly and straight but you're still not satisfied with the distance, you need to check to see if your wrists are sufficiently flexed during the backswing. During a golf swing, your wrists turn your arms and the club into a two-lever system which increases the speed of the clubhead dramatically. The degree of flexion of your wrists determines the speed of the clubhead. In other words, if you bend your wrists more, you increase the speed. In order to do that, you must have a proper grip. If, for instance, the pad of your left hand doesn't sufficiently cover the grip from above, you'll find it almost impossible to bend your wrists. Therefore, you have to hold the club from the left side of your body and make sure that the pad of your left hand is far enough up towards the end of the grip so

that, when viewed from the front, your hand covers all of the grip.

In addition, you should not hold on to the club too tightly because this could cause muscle cramps in your wrist. Now, during the backswing, you can bend your wrists so that at the highest point of the backswing you create a 135-degree angle between your left arm and the club.

If you hold the club properly, your hand completely covers the top portion of the grip.

Bending your wrists during the backswing creates an angle between your arm and the club of up to 130 degrees.

Insufficient Body Tension

Characteristics
- Insufficient shoulder rotation (shanks, slices, pulls)
- Exaggerated hip rotation (heel of left foot raised off ground during backswing)

The second reason for a lack speed of the clubhead is an incorrect body rotation. As is the case when you throw a ball, the movement during the backswing creates tension between the upper and lower half of your body. The more the upper half of your body rotates, and the less the lower half follows this rotation, the more tension you create in your whole body. This body tension determines the speed of the clubhead.

Two problems are responsible for insufficient body tension: either your shoulders don't rotate enough or your hips rotate too much. When trying to reduce the rotation of your hips, make sure that you are not also reducing the rotation of your shoulders, or you won't change a thing. At the highest point of the backswing, your shoulders must have rotated 90 degrees in relation to the address position.

In addition, the club must point in the direction of the target, or it will approach the ball from the outside, reducing the distance even more than the distance gained by increasing body tension.

One way of reducing hip rotation is to turn your right foot slightly to the inside. This reduces the ability of the lower half of your body to rotate, leading to more tension. In addition to too much hip rotation and too little shoulder rotation, two additional problems may create a lack of tension between the upper and lower body. Your hips may move too strongly to the right, or they may shift too far in the direction of the target during the backswing.

During a neutral swing, the hips ought to be slightly to the right at the beginning of the movement of the backswing. Immediately before the end, they shift to the left. If, however, the hips move to the right and outside during the backswing, the side movement will be too strong, and your upper body cannot shift sideways without losing balance. If your hips shift to the left or outside at the start of the backswing movement, you are unable to put your whole weight behind the ball during the downswing. The club will approach the ball too steeply, or

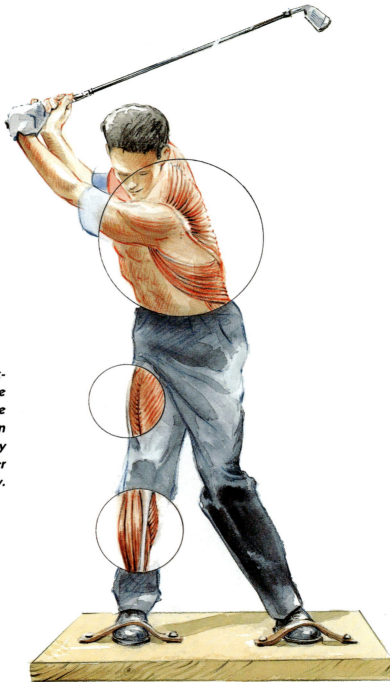

During the back-swing, you have to create muscle tension between the upper body and the lower body.

Shifting your hips reduces the resistance that the upper body needs in order to create tension through rotation.

If your hips move out of the way during the back-swing, you can-not center your body over your right foot.

you will have to compensate by moving towards the right during the downswing, which will not greatly increase the speed of the clubhead.

To correct both of these mistakes, try this exercise. First, push a golf club into the ground. The club should be in an upright position that reaches up to your hip to the right of your right foot. Leave a space of about 2 inches (5 cm) between your hip and the shaft of the club. You need this space because your stance is wider than your hips, so your right leg isn't perfectly

THE LONG GAME

During a neutral swing, your hips move only a bit to the side, so you build up maximum tension between the upper and lower body.

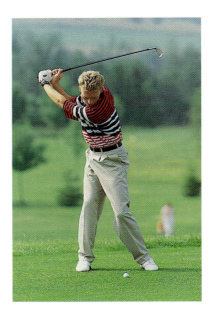

Reasons for Insufficient Distance

▶ *Speed of the clubhead is sufficient, but shots are bad: open clubface, missed sweet spot, wrong angle at moment of impact.*

▶ *Your wrists are not bent enough towards the side of the thumb, and the speed of your hands cannot increase sufficiently during the downswing.*

▶ *Insufficient muscle tension between your upper and lower body because of lack of shoulder rotation or too much hip rotation during the backswing.*

▶ *During the backswing, hips shifted too far to the right or moved out to the left.*

straight. When your club passes the 90-degree angle in the backswing, your hips can move only as far to the right as the club shaft in the ground allows. Immediately before the end of the backswing, your hips may move to the left away from the shaft.

Underhitting

The reason for underhitting is seldom that you have teed off too high, but that your swing was too steep at the moment of impact. If the club hits the ball from above instead of from behind, the upper edge of the clubhead drives the ball vertically into the air.

Underhit balls that are in good position on the fairway indicate that the problem cannot only be the result of a high tee-off. We will discuss three causes for approaching the ball too steeply at the moment of impact.

Underhitting from the Outside

Characteristics
- Pulls and slices
- Divots pointing clearly to the left
- Topped balls to the left
- Good hits with short irons

As we stated in the chapter on slices, the path of a swing moving from the outside in at the moment of impact always creates an angle that is too steep. Underhitting because the club approaches the ball too much from the outside is usually not the only problem. Underhits frequently happen along with slices and/or pulls. If that is the case, use the correction that we mentioned for the classic slice, plateau slice, and pull, and you will eliminate underhitting from the outside at the same time.

A ball is usually underhit when the approach is too steep and it is hit with the upper edge, not because it is played too high off the tee.

Underhitting Due to Steep Swing Plane

Characteristics
- *High push slice*
- *Hitting with tip*
- *Hitting with too much ground*
- *Good hits with short irons*

When your arms and the golf club move too high during the backswing, meaning they move on a plane that is too steep, they will go too far down during the downswing. This type of movement is the same as that of the modern slice. For a correction, we suggest that you practice baseball swings and swings from a position in which the ball is higher than your feet. The rounder your swing is, the less you need to be afraid that the club will reach the ball too low, creating an underhit. You then do not need to try to tee off very low.

Underhitting Due to Reverse Pivot

Characteristics
- *Slices*
- *Deep divots*
- *Problems with balance during the swing*
- *Good hits with irons, bad hits with woods*

If your spine leans to the left during the backswing, your body's center of gravity shifts too far to the left. You don't even have to move your head to the left for that to happen, because the spine shifts to the left even when the head does not change its position during the backswing.

If, however, your spine is

If the arms move too steeply and far up during the backswing, they will also swing too steeply and low during the downswing.

If the center of gravity at the highest point of the backswing is too far left, the approach is also too steep.

stationary, your head will move slightly to the right during the backswing. Note that if your spine is already moving to the left during the backswing, this automatic shifting to the left in the forward movement ensures that your body's center of gravity is shifting to the left at the moment of impact. The result is that the club is too steep at the moment of impact. These factors are not very important when using an iron. The only effects are deep divots and a minimal loss of distance. You will, however, lose a lot of distance when you underhit with a wood.

And as is the case with a reverse pivot slice, practicing with the ball higher than your feet works well. During the backswing, gravity automatically pulls your body to the right, preventing your body from shifting to the left. In this way, the club approaches the ball at a much flatter plane during the downswing.

Instead of a wood, use a medium iron when teeing off with the ball in an uphill position. Immediately following this—and here is the trick—tee off with a wood from a level position. When hitting with an iron from an elevated situation, the angle of impact is precisely the proper one for hitting with a wood from a tee.

Reasons for Underhitting

▶ *The angle of impact is always too steep. Teeing off too high is never the only reason.*
▶ *The path of the swing moves too much from the outside in.*
▶ *The plane of the swing of the club and/or your arms is too steep.*
▶ *Your body is shifting too far to the left during the backswing and at the moment of impact.*

Pulling

A pulled ball starts to the left, continues straight, and then lands to the left of the target. In order to recognize and avoid pulling the ball, make sure that the ball is actually starting out to the left of the target and not simply in the direction left of the target. The latter may also be the result of unintentionally aiming to the left of the target, in which case the swing might be correct.

Pulls from the Outside

Characteristics
- Good hits with short irons
- Problems with long clubs
- Divots point too far to left and are too deep
- Slices with the longer clubs
- Underhitting when teeing off

When you pull a long ball, you swing the club through the ball from the outside in, and the clubface is at a right angle to the ball. In other words, the clubface is closed in relation to the line to the target. If you are only pulling shots with short or medium irons and slicing shots with long irons or woods, all you need to correct is the path of the outside-in swing and not the closed clubface.

Make sure that the ball is not too close to your left foot. Because of sufficient body rotation, the club should point to the target or slightly to the right of it at the highest point of the backswing. During the downswing, concentrate on moving your arms down without much body rotation.

After you have made the correction, hit a few practice shots exclusively from a tee, because the angle of impact of the club has become flatter during the exercises, and you need a couple of hits to get used to the idea.

THE LONG GAME

Pulling with a Correct Swing Curve

Characteristics
- *Pull hooks*
- *Hits too flat*
- *Normal divots*

Reasons for Pulling

....

▶ *Pulls from the outside: ball played too much off your left foot or the club points too far to the left and past the target during the backswing.*

▶ *Pulls with a correct swing: as with hooks, the problem is a closed clubface.*

▶ *Worn balls that contaminate the results of shot.*

....

Hitting with short irons or with a reduced clubhead speed can also lead to pulling the ball, even when the path of the swing does not necessarily move from the outside in. If the path is correct, but the clubface is closed, the ball will start out going to the left and, under normal circumstances, will also veer to the left. With a short iron, the sidespin is often minute because of the low point of impact and the reduced speed of the clubhead. Thus, the ball veers to the left only a little or not at all. If that is the case, other hits are more likely to be hooked than sliced. With longer clubs, this can only happen when you use balls that are extremely worn, because a ball without dimples has very little backspin.

If this is the reason you are pulling, you must correct the closed clubface. You can find the possible reasons you are doing this in the chapter on hooks.

Pushing

A push is the opposite of a pull. In other words, the reason for the mistake and the subsequent correction need to be reversed. This means a pushed ball starts out to the right of the direction you have lined up, flies straight, and lands to the right of the line to the target. In order to recognize and correct a push, you must make sure that your balls are actually veering to the right and not only in the direction that is to the right of the target. The latter could simply be the result of unintentionally lining up to the right of the target.

In the case of a long push, for instance anything over 165 to 220 yards (150-200m), the path of the swing moves from the inside out. The clubface is at a right angle to the path of the swing and, in relation to the intended line to the target, is open. If you are only pushing when you use short or medium irons and you hook when you use long irons and woods, you must correct the inside-out path but not the open clubface. Try placing the ball close to your right foot and moving so that at the highest point of the backswing the club points directly to or slightly to the left of the target. During the downswing, concentrate on moving the club in front of the body, not too far back.

Correct the push by inserting a tee into the end of the grip. Make sure it points forward to the right instead of to the right and back.

Pushing from the Inside Out

Characteristics
- *Problem with short clubs*
- *Divots to right of ball pointing to right*
- *Problems hitting out of the rough and hitting from bald spots*
- *Hooks with long clubs*

89

THE LONG GAME

Pushing with a Correct Swing

Characteristics
- *Push slice*
- *Hits too high*
- *Normal divots*

These pushes usually occur when you use a short iron or when the speed of the clubhead is very slow. In this case, the path of the swing is not from the inside out. If the path of the swing is correct, but the clubface is open, the following will happen: the ball will start out to the right, and under normal circumstances will also veer off to the right.

When using a short iron, however, the sidespin is often minimal because of the low impact point and the slow speed of the clubhead, and, thus, the ball veers only a little or not at all to the right. Your other shots may not hook but slice. Such a push only happens with long clubs when the balls are very worn and unable to spin.

If this is the reason you are pushing your balls, you have to correct the angle of the clubface. We discussed the possible reasons for this and suggested exercises to eliminate the problem in the chapter on slices.

Reasons for Pushing

....

▶ *Pushing from the inside: playing the ball too close to your right foot or pointing the club too far to the right during the backswing.*

▶ *Pushing with the correct swing: as in the case of the slice, the problem is the open clubface.*

▶ *Balls with worn dimples can add problems.*

....

Hitting Too High and Too Flat

If you believe your balls are not getting high enough in the air, make sure not to fall into the trap called exaggerated perfectionism. When analyzing a bad round, you will rarely learn that your balls were flying too high or too flat. Usually, they were hit wrong or veered off in the wrong direction. If you are basically happy with the results of your game, don't change your swing. This will only make things worse.

Before you start searching for reasons that your balls are not flying properly, you should know the following:

1. Very few clubs are sold with the proper loft and lie. You can bend most irons afterwards. If balls hit with a specific club fly too high or too flat, go back to the pro who sold the club for possible corrections.

2. A ball played too close off the left or right foot will fly too high or too flat, respectively. Make use of this fact when you want to hit a ball high or flat. Since an improper direction distorts the position of the ball, place a golf club in front of your feet and a second club vertical to the first, pointing to the ball. This allows you to find the right position for the ball.

3. You can only judge how high a ball flies when you hit a straight shot. If you are slicing consistently, the ball will fly too high; if you are hooking, the ball will have a flatter flight curve than a straight ball.

4. In conclusion, when judging the height of a ball, you must also consider the distance of your hits. A player who hits the ball twice as far as another player will also hit a ball twice as high (depending on the club). In other words, if you are a long hitter, you will also hit the balls higher; if your hits are short, they will usually also be flatter.

If you are still under the impression that your balls are flying too high or too flat, we'll discuss a number of possible reasons on the following pages.

Grip and Release

Golfers who are able to hit a straight ball do not necessarily always have a neutral technique. Hitting a straight shot is often a matter of several mistakes canceling each other

Hands rotated too far to the right on the grip result in a hooked ball. . . .

out. If, for instance, you have a hook factor in your swing, you may make up for it with a slice factor on a later shot. While the clubface approaches the ball straight on, your hands are way ahead of the ball. This considerably reduces the angle of the club. The result is a ball that will fly on a flat curve. If you have a pair of mistakes, you have to eliminate both, or the ball won't fly straight.

. . . Often, you instinctively compensate with a later hit. However, with your hands too far ahead of the ball at the moment of impact, the loft is considerably reduced.

93

A golfer who has a higher handicap usually shows other variations, such as one or more slice factors. For instance, in the case of a slice grip, the golfer may compensate with a

If your hands rotate too far to the left on the grip, you will ordinarily slice the ball. . . .

spooned hit in which the club-head reaches the ball ahead of the hands, increasing the loft and giving the ball more height.

In this case, too, both mistakes need to be dealt with at the same time. High handicappers should first eliminate the slice factor, so that they will start to hook, before they attempt to bring their hands into a better position, which in turn will give the ball a flatter flight curve.

... You often instinctively compensate with an early hit, but your hands are ahead of the ball at the moment of impact, considerably increasing the loft.

Body Position at Moment of Impact

Another reason for the flight curve to be either too high or too flat is a faulty body position at the moment of impact. If your body is too far to the left at the moment of impact, you rob your club of its loft, and the flight curve will be flat.

To correct this, you need to practice from an uphill position. Your body's gravity makes it impossible to fall to the left too early, and this uphill position is helpful in developing a feeling for the right movement. After a period of practice, this body position will feel normal on a flat surface.

If your body is too far to the right at the moment of impact, the club has too much loft, and the ball will fly too high. Here, you must practice hitting in the downhill position because gravity pulls your body to the left during the downswing.

If your body is shifted too far left, with too much weight on your left foot at impact, every ball will have a flat flight path. . . .

. . . *If your body weight is still on your right foot at the moment of impact, the ball will fly too high.*

Arm Plane

An improper arm plane also influences the height of the ball. The steeper the arm plane, the higher the balls will fly; and the flatter the arm plane, the flatter the flight path will be. To correct this, hit from a position in which the ball is above your feet. This flattens the arm plane. The reverse also works. In order to increase the arm plane, hit from a position in which the ball is below your feet.

Reasons for High Flat Hits

....

▶ *The club has the wrong loft, you are not playing the ball from a proper position, or the ball does not fly straight.*

▶ *The reason a ball flies too high may be an early hit or a hit from an arm plane that is too steep. If the body is too far behind the ball at the moment of impact, the ball will fly too high.*

▶ *The reason the ball flies too flat may be a late hit or a flat arm plane. If your body is too far to the left at the moment of impact, the ball will fly too high.*

....

Hitting downhill causes your weight to shift to the left earlier and more decisively during the backswing.

MISTAKES IN THE SHORT GAME

You'll find that corrections to improve your short game are much more successful than those for your long game. They require less energy and less mobility, and the techniques are simpler.

Pitching

A pitch is just a smaller version of a full swing. Therefore, the mistakes you make during the long game and the pitch are similar. Golfers who move their driver back on a flat curve will also do so with the sand wedge. However, the same mistake made during a shot with a long club has different effects than those for a short club. For instance, hitting off the tee, the path of the swing from the inside out with a flat vertical angle is not all that much of a problem. In the case of a high approach shot, however, that same swing would be disastrous.

Backswing Too Flat

Characteristics
- *Pushed pitches*
- *Divots too far right or absent altogether (thin hits)*
- *Shanks (sockets)*

With the exception of the putter, the wedge is the club with the steepest angle, and the goal is to maximize the backspin rather than to increase the length of the hit. For that reason, the wedge, more than any other club, must approach the ball at a steeper angle. That, however, cannot happen if the club and your arms are moving too far behind your body during the backswing.

Often the reason for this mistake in the short game is that you line up incorrectly. Usually, we recommend an open foot position for pitching. You place your left foot farther back. However, many players find it difficult to move only the lower half of the left side of their body, and they usually shift their whole body towards the left.

Shifting your body to the left when pitching makes it difficult to bring the club back into the proper path . . .

. . . and forces
you to pull the
club back too far
to the inside.
The result is that
the club moves
too far forward
during the down-
swing.

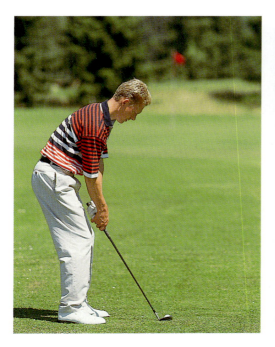 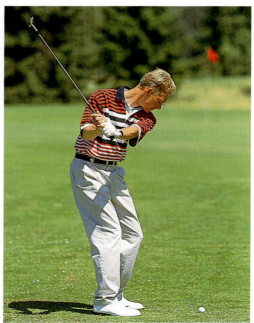

A ball hit neutrally from this position will land to the left of the target. Instinctively, the whole plane of the swing tilts to the right, and the club swings too far back in relation to the body.

The vertex of the swing then shifts to the right, and the result is either a fat hit or thin hit. Such swing curves make it almost impossible for you to hit a divot to the left of the ball.

In addition, a club that moves too far back during the backswing tends to make the downswing come too far forward, hitting the ball with the heel of the clubhead. In order to correct this situation, line up straight ahead, swing the club back with only a little lower arm rotation, and use a lot of wrist action.

Make sure, however, that you have sufficient shoulder rotation throughout. Otherwise this could lead to a different form of shank.

When pitching, use a direct line to the target (left) . . .

. . . so that you can bring the club back in the proper, steeper plane (right).

Insufficient Use of the Wrists

Characteristics
- *Thin hits*
- *Weak balls, often short distance only*
- *High balls with little backspin*

If your wrists are not properly flexed during the backswing, the club does not reach high enough and often approaches the ball at a too flat angle. . . .

In order to create sufficient clubhead speed and a vertical angle at the moment of impact to provide the ball with a sufficient amount of backspin, you must bend your wrists towards the side of your thumb when you pitch. If you don't, the clubhead doesn't move high enough during the backswing and, in turn, the clubhead does not come down far enough during the downswing. The result is that the club hits the ball above the equator.

If you hit a shot cleanly with this technique, the flat angle at the moment of impact will force the ball to fly very high, but it will have little backspin. The curve of the flight considerably shortens the distance of the hit. In order to remedy this situation, first check out how tight your grip on the club is. Extreme tension in your hands stiffens your wrists and makes it impossible to bend them properly. Before you actually hit the ball, lift the club off the ground several times, using only your wrists. This exercise will also improve the use of your wrists during the swing.

When hitting, concentrate on bending your wrists towards the thumb so that your left arm and the shaft of the club will be at a right angle to the ground. When you try to correct this situation, your first couple of hits will usually go too far, but don't unbend your wrists again and don't reduce the follow-through. Instead, reduce the length of the arm swing of the backswing. If, in the beginning, the club penetrates too far into the ground, try to make yourself smaller, so that you feel as if you can hit the divot with your whole body. If, however, a steeper club position is responsible for creating the divot, then using your body becomes unnecessary and, after some practice, the problem will disappear.

. . . Before the actual hit, practice lifting the club off the ground a few times using only your wrists. It will help the club get into the air faster during the backswing.

THE SHORT GAME

If your back-swing is too long for a particular distance, you will need to shorten the follow-through unnaturally.

Backswing Too Long

Characteristics
- Short follow-through
- Problem getting swing length right

When pitching, the amount of backswing determines the flight distance of the ball. Always use a complete follow-through.

For pitching, even more than for chipping, you must not break the swing as the club moves through the ball. Getting a feeling for the proper length of a swing is easiest if you practice with three different lengths of backswing, using the same full follow-through for each.

Using extra-long backswings is common because the club usually travels much farther back than you are aware of. In the beginning, if you force yourself to consistently use a full follow-through when pitching, the ball may go too far. However, after a short period of time, your backswing will become shorter on its own.

For this type of correction, using a video camera can be very helpful.

If you try to push the club under the ball, all you get is a spooning movement.

Characteristics
- Balls fly too high
- Thin, topped, and fat hits
- Balls are hit with the tip
- Balls veer off to the left

Many golfers believe that their club has to hit under the ball (spoon) in order for the ball to be airborne. But this would only be necessary if golfers

For pitching, the club must move down and through the ball, hitting the divot after the moment of impact.

used clubs shaped like hockey sticks, which have no loft.

Even if, for instance, you want to hit a ball high in the air with a putter, you won't need this type of approach. When you swing down, however, you must hit the ball with the lower edge of the club below the equator, because the angle is 50–60 degrees. The distinct upward movement of the club at the moment of impact leads to a clear divot that points to the left of the ball.

In order to hit a shot with a downward swing, both your hands must be in front of the ball at the moment of impact. The back of your left hand and your lower left arm are one continuous line.

While practicing, make sure that you hit a divot to the left of the ball. Don't cheat. While swinging from the outside in would give you the same results, it would be going in the wrong direction and would not lead to the same success. Instead, practice with half hits, stopping shortly after the moment of impact to check if your left arm and the club are in a straight line.

For the club to be moving down at the moment of impact, the back of hand and forearm should form a straight line.

Reasons for Bad Pitches

▶ *Moving the club back on a plane that is too flat creates pushing, fat and thin hits, and/or shanks.*

▶ *Not bending your wrists sufficiently during the backswing and a late angle at the moment of impact result in thin hits or balls that start out too high, have little backspin, and fall short of the target.*

▶ *An extremely long backswing makes it difficult to find the proper movement for pitching because it requires a breaking motion during the forward movement.*

▶ *Spooning movements at the moment of impact result in shots that are too high, thin, or fat, or that veer off to the left. They also result in balls hit with the tip of the clubhead.*

THE SHORT GAME

Bunker Shots

Wrong Positioning and Wrong Swing Plane

Most golfers know that for a standard bunker shot the clubface must be wide open. From that they assume that they must place themselves as far to the left as the clubface points to the right. Here are four reasons why that is not necessary:

1. In the bunker, the club makes no contact with the ball. The amount of sand pushed ahead of the club neutralizes the rotation somewhat because the amount of sand at the tip of the club is greater than that at the heel.

2. The wedge closes effortlessly since the sand breaks the momentum of the club earlier and more forcefully at the heel than at the tip.

3. Because the ball sits far to the left of the vertex of the arch of the swing, the club moves to the inside at the moment of impact (to the left), and the clubface is already slightly closed at the moment of impact.

4. Even if you hit the shot in the grass instead of in the bunker, the ball would only get about 75 percent of the distance it would get from a normal address position.

Even when the
clubface is wide
open, you don't
need to aim to
the left in the
bunker. Doing so
only leads to the
wrong swing
plane.

Even when the clubface is wide open, the ball starts only minimally to the right of the swing plane.

In other words, if you position yourself as far to the left of the target as the clubface points to the right, the ball will certainly land to the left of the target. In no more than two hits, you will react to this and begin to aim more to the right. However, this is wrong and seldom corrects the problem. A swing path from the inside out causes the club to hit into the sand too early and, depending on the position of the clubface, will either bury the sand wedge too deeply or simply bounce off and hit the ball too high.

The proper way to set up depends on several factors. If the clubface is open at a 30 degree angle, your stance should never be more than 5 percent to the left of the target. In other words, open the clubface wide to allow the sand wedge to slide through the sand easily. Make sure that you play the ball convincingly more from the left foot so that the club hits the sand before the ball, and line yourself up only slightly to the left of the target.

Insufficient Follow-Through

Characteristics
- Shot-guage problems
- Backswing movement too extreme
- Shortened forward movement (club gets stuck in sand)

A unique problem exists when playing out of the bunker. You may end your follow-through too early because you experience an unfamiliar resistance before the moment of impact. While this resistance doesn't necessarily influence the actual hit, you store the experience, and the next time you hit a bunker shot, you simply reach farther back. A more consistent follow-through would be better. Just as is true with a pitch, you need to balance the follow-through against the extent of the backswing.

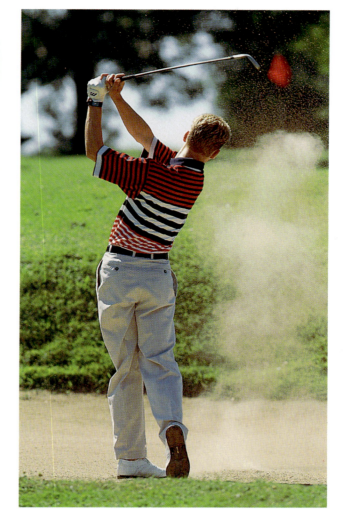

In a bunker, a complete follow-through is especially important so that the club is not buried in the sand.

Spooning

Characteristics
- *Very bad bunker shots: the club hits the sand too early or hits the ball too high and the ball flies beyond the green*
- *No sense of gauging shots*

If you haven't quite mastered the downswing yet and your club is already moving upwards at the moment of impact, you won't have much of a problem in the fairway, particularly when you have lined up well. In a bunker, however, you ought to leave yourself more room. If the deepest point of the swing is too far to the right of the ball, and the club hits the sand too early, the momentum of the club breaks too early and you cannot lift the ball over the edge of the bunker. When the club bounces off and hits the ball too high, you'll find yourself playing out of the bunker on the opposite side of the green. This is not a useful technique and, usually, you cannot correct it in the bunker. For that reason, you should deal first with your pitching mistakes. Thanks to the simpler hitting techniques, you'll have a much easier time determining if you hit the ball properly simply by following the flight of the ball and by reading the divot (see page 102: "Pitching"). If you have corrected your pitching mistakes, practice in the bunker by hitting balls buried in the sand. Here, the club needs to approach at a very

A long follow-through prevents a spooning movement. Therefore, in the bunker, use it to practice hitting balls buried in the sand.

steep angle, and the follow-through has to be particularly good. If you have mastered these hits, you will also successfully hit out of the bunker in a normal situation.

Reasons for Bad Bunker Shots

▶ An open stance that quickly leads to lining up to the left of the target, making it necessary to swing from the inside out, complicating the technique.

▶ An inconsistent follow-through in the bunker increases the amount of the backswing and makes it impossible to consistently gauge the situation.

▶ Spooning the ball in the bunker leads to fat and thin hits. The first order of business is to correct your pitching technique.

Chipping

The chip is the easiest approach shot, and very few golfers have any difficulty with it. The most frequent problems involve properly gauging the situation so that you make clean contact with the ball.

Too Much Backswing

Characteristics
- Assessment problems
- Insufficient follow-through

As is the case when throwing a bocce ball, the approach depends on one rule: the follow-through must be longer than the backswing.

In golf, if the club moves too far back, you cannot consistently increase the speed of the forward movement, or you would hit the ball too far. The result is that you break the movement just before the moment of impact. In turn, that makes it difficult to gauge the swing and hit the ball cleanly. Therefore, you should only move the club back until you think that the backswing would be too short for the distance that you want the ball to fly. This forces you to control the movement of the club during the downswing.

Most players have the wrong idea of how far the club really moves back during the backswing. The actual distance is much longer. This exercise is worthwhile: Place a basket at the position and height where you want your backswing to end and hit a few chips. Make a few slow practice swings to determine that the basket is in the right place. The first few times you try to hit the ball, you will hit the basket instead. Once you are successful in carrying out practice hits without hitting the basket, however, you will know that your backswing, your downswing, and your follow-through are all the same length. You will most likely feel as if you have barely reached back and that your downswing and follow-through are considerably longer. Don't be confused; try to carry this feeling with you when you swing without a basket.

When throwing a bocce ball, the follow-through will cover a greater distance than the wind-up.

Backswing Is Too Flat

Characteristics
- *Pushed chips*
- *Difficulty brushing club over the grass to the left of the ball*
- *Shanks (sockets)*

If your club swings back too far to the inside, the vertex of the swing curve moves to the right. The result is fat and thin chips, and it becomes almost impossible to brush the grass with the club to the left of the ball. In addition, the club has a tendency to move forward during the downswing when swinging too far back during the backswing. As a result, you hit the ball with the heel of the club.

This mistake is easy to correct when chipping. Place a cardboard box or something similar in a position that you will hit with the club if you move the club back too far. During the backswing and the downswing, the clubhead travels so slowly that you can easily practice this exercise with a basket. The advantage of this exercise is that you will immediately recognize whether or not the club is moving on the wrong path. All you need to do once you've established the correct path is to make sure that the club travels on the same path during the downswing.

To compensate for a previous mistake, players often try to move the club in a kind of looping movement during the downswing in order to bring the club back onto the correct path. This is unnecessary, and you can correct this with the help of a second box or carton that you place in front of the ball but outside of the line to the target.

Spooning

Characteristics
- Balls fly too high
- Thin and topped hits
- Fat hits

Moving the club in a spooning motion is even less necessary in chipping than it is in pitching because a chip should not hit the ball into the air much at all. However, golfers who tend to spoon almost all other hits will most certainly carry this habit through when chipping.

When chipping, the club moves slightly down at the moment of impact.

121

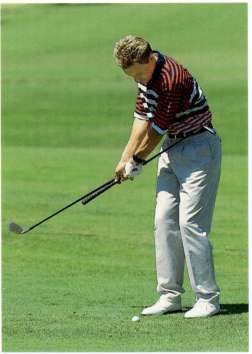

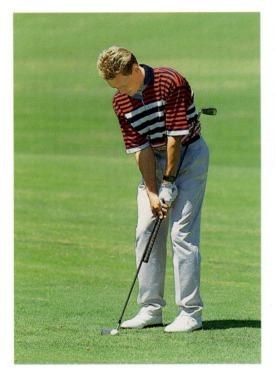

. . . *use a second club as an aid.*

In order to hit down, you must not bend your left wrist in the direction of the back of your hand during the downswing. Here is a wonderful exercise for chipping: lengthen your club by adding a second club, as shown in the picture. Make a few practice swings first, and then start the real chipping.

This exercise prevents your wrist from bending because the second club blocks your body.

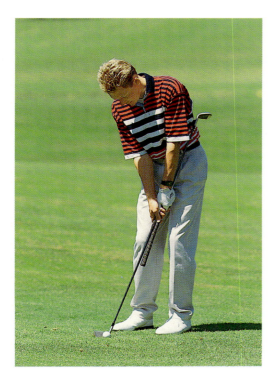
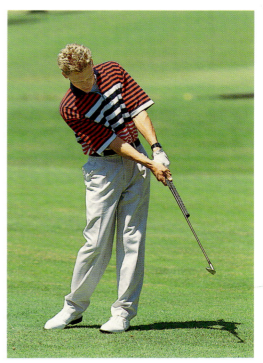

Reasons for Bad Chips

....

▶ *When you move back too far during the backswing, you have a difficult time gauging and adjusting the forward movement.*
▶ *A swing plane that is too flat leads to pushing, fat and thin hits, and/or shanks.*
▶ *Spooning the club at the moment of impact leads to hits that are too high, thin, and fat.*

....

Putting

Technical mistakes are less obvious when putting. Every now and then you can make exceptional putts, even when you use a totally unorthodox and faulty technique. In order to better assess your game, analyze a round after you have completed it. If your putting score is too high, look at your putting technique and examine the mistakes you made.

Sad to say, in contrast to other approach shots the corrections you make in your putting technique seldom show immediate results and improvements. You'll need some time before unfamiliar techniques become habit. However, training diligently will pay off over time, and the result is more consistency with your putting.

Ineffective Training

Characteristics
- *No improvement in putting seen immediately after practice*
- *No improvement in putting over time*

Most golfers only practice their putting just before they play a round. Even those who consistently practice more do not necessarily use this time very productively. As a rule, they go to the putting green and hit three balls into different holes over and over again. This method has three disad-

 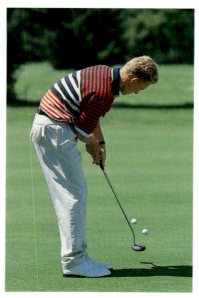

vantages: it doesn't do much to improve your sense of distance, it doesn't do anything to improve your ability to read a green, and it doesn't improve your technique.

These exercises are indispensable to get results from your putting practice. Place two balls next to each other in front of your putter. Each should be the same distance from the putter. Now, without aiming at a hole, putt as you normally would for a 15-foot (5m) putt. If your putter is exactly vertical to the line to the target at the moment of impact, you will hit both balls simultaneously, and they will roll next to each other at equal speeds. If the putter rotates to

Using two balls when you practice putting lets you determine if the club approaches the ball straight on or rotates at the moment of impact.

the left at the moment of impact, you'll hit the ball on the outside (right) first. This ball will roll ahead of and farther than the ball on the inside.

If the club rotates to the right at the moment of impact, you'll hit the ball on the inside

Place a ball slightly beyond the club tip and a second slightly behind to find out if you are hitting the middle ball with the sweet spot.

(left) first, and it will roll ahead of and farther than the ball on the outside. Depending on the distance between the two balls, you can gauge how severely the putter rotated at the moment of impact.

The sweet spot is extremely important because it is difficult to improve your technique when you hit the ball badly and it reacts differently each time. Here is another exercise that lets you practice hitting the ball with the sweet spot. In order to determine which part of the putter has hit the ball, place one ball ¼ inch (½cm) in front of the tip and a second ball ¼ inch (½cm) behind the heel of the putter. Remove the putter and place a third ball where the sweet spot of the putter is. At this point, you have three balls lined up in a row.

Now, without aiming at a hole, try to putt the center ball 15 feet (5m). If you hit the center ball with the sweet spot, the two other balls will remain untouched. However, if you hit the ball in the middle with the heel of the club, you will also hit the ball located at the tip of the club. On the other hand, if you hit more with the tip, you'll also hit the ball behind the heel. This exercise will show you immediately what has gone wrong. Learning to gauge your hits properly will help improve your aim considerably.

If you want to start putting into a hole immediately after these exercises, use only one ball and take your time reading the green before putting.

·If you have practiced putting a hole with two balls, gauging your hits and recognizing the proper putting line won't be difficult.

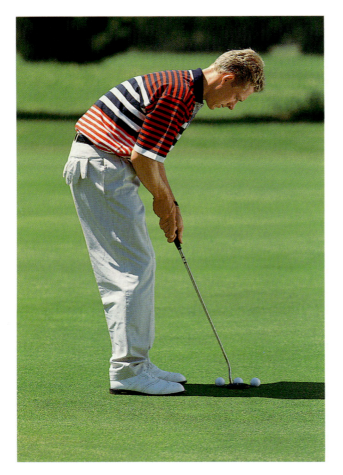

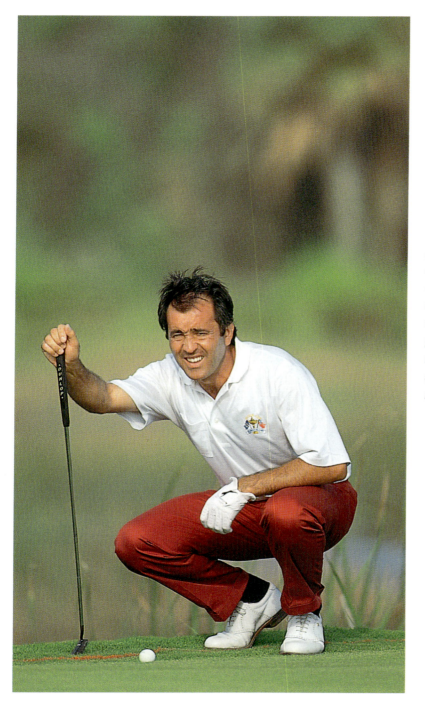

Read the green carefully to identify the correct putting line and the proper amount of force needed for the shot. Both pieces of information help in avoiding putting mistakes.

Most players position the putter at too flat an angle; the putter is too far from the ball and the eyes cannot see the intended line to the target.

Improper Setup

Characteristics
- *Tip of putter is lifted up*
- *Distance to ball is too great*

Most players hold a putter the same as any other club. This is a mistake because the putter has a totally different lie. If you hold a putter as you would any other club, you have a very difficult time placing the sole of the putter on the ground properly. When putting, you must hold the grip of the club with your hand pad and thumb pad. If you use any other hold, the angle of the shaft will be too flat, and the ball too far away.

When you use an improper grip, you take your eyes off the intended line to the target, making it very difficult to set up properly. In addition, an improper grip leads to an improper use of your wrists. That, in turn, makes gauging your putt a game of chance. If, on the other hand, you hold the club so that the end of the grip is between the pad of the hand and the thumb, you increase the angle of the shaft, and the result is that your lower arm and the putter shaft (viewed from the side) are in one line.

In this way, the whole sole of the putter rests on the ground properly. You are so

To place the putter on the ground properly, you must hold the club on one side. Which hand you place on top is unimportant.

129

In the proper position, your lower arm and the shaft of the club are aligned. Your eyes can focus on the line to the target.

Path of the Swing Is Incorrect

In spite of getting in the proper position, many players move the putt along a wrong path. Because for their long shots they usually swing the golf club on a circular path in which the clubface opens and closes, they may use this kind of circular swing when putting.

Because you don't rotate your shoulders during putting, your lower arms remain pas-

close to the ball that your eyes can easily focus on the line to the target. This grip also allows your wrists to be more passive. You gauge the putt exclusively by the tilting, pendulum-like movement of the shoulders.

The incorrect use of the body (rotating instead of tilting) leads to the wrong position during the follow-through.

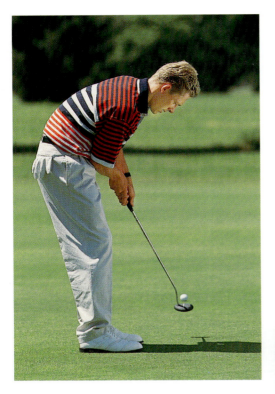

Simply tilting your shoulders moves the putter in a straight line, and the clubface remains at a right angle to the line to the target until the end.

This putting track is ideal for learning to swing the putter along the proper path.

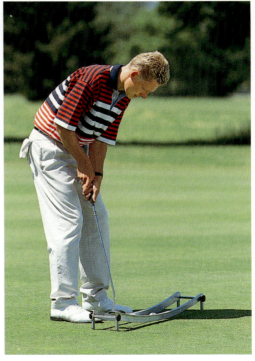

sive. In the correct address position, your hands are underneath your shoulders. The club has to move on a straight path, and the clubface must always remain at a right angle to the line to the target.

To ensure that your putter moves straight, practice this shoulder tilt on the so-called putting track. If you cannot locate one, use two wooden poles. Place them next to each other, making sure that you leave sufficient space between them. Training sessions are most effective when you adjust the exercise equipment in such a way that you guarantee a success rate of about fifty percent. If your success rate after a while is eighty percent, adjust the equipment so that you are back at a fifty percent success rate.

Reasons for Bad Putting

······································

▶ *Haphazard putting with three balls from hole to hole instead of practicing the factors involved at the moment of impact.*
▶ *Neglecting to practice reading the putting line on the green.*
▶ *Holding the putter like other golf clubs so that you cannot place it on the ground properly, the ball is too far away, and your eyes are unable to stay on the line to the target.*
▶ *Swinging from the inside out with the clubface opening and closing instead of tilting your shoulders like a pendulum.*

······································

GLOSSARY

*This helpful listing
explains the ideas and
terms used in golf.*

the path of the club immediately before the moment of impact. (You can only observe this from the front.)

Backspin: The rotation of the ball around its own axis against the direction of the flight. (Every ball in flight has backspin, otherwise it would fall back to the ground immediately.) Backspin is not just a factor after the ball hits the ground, but if the ball rolls back, it has a particularly strong backspin. The loft of the clubhead creates backspin.

Bulge: The horizontally rounded clubface of a wood.

Carry: Distance the ball is actually in the air, not including the distance that it rolls on the ground.

Centrifugal force: The force caused by the rotation of an object around a point from the center to the outside.

Chip: A flat approach shot.

Club

closed: When viewed from the end of the handle, the club rotates counterclockwise. The terms flat and steep refer to the shaft of the club during the swing. The terms open and closed refer to the clubface. The terms open and closed are somewhat confusing since an

Address position: The position of the golfer after he has assumed his stance and positioned his club.

Angle at impact: The horizontal and vertical angle of the clubhead at the moment of impact:

The horizontal angle at the moment of impact is the angle of the club between the intended line to the target and the horizontal component of the path of the club just prior to impact. (You can only observe this from the side.)

The vertical angle of impact is the angle between the ground and the vertical component of

open stance indicates an alignment too far to the left of the target, and an open clubface refers to the fact that the club turns to the right.

flat: The clubhead points to a particular spot within the intended line to the target, or the grip of the club points to a spot outside of the intended line to the target. (If the shaft is parallel to the ground, the club points to the right of the target.)

open: When viewed from the end of the grip, the club rotates clockwise.

steep: The head of the shaft of the club points to a spot outside the intended line to the target, or the grip points at a spot inside the intended line to the target. (If the shaft is parallel to the ground, the club points to the left of the target.)

Divot: A piece of grass cut out with a club.

Dorsal flexion: Bending the wrist in the direction of the back of the hand.

Downswing: The part of the swing starting at the end of the backswing and continuing to the moment of impact.

Draw: A shot that starts out to the right of the target and then veers slightly to the left. (This is the opposite of a fade.)

Explosion shot: A bunker shot in which the player deliberately hits the sand before hitting the ball. The club hits a slice of sand underneath the ball, forcing the ball to fly out of the bunker. The sand flies out of the bunker like an explosion.

Fade: A shot that starts out to the left of the target and then veers slightly to the right. (This is the opposite of a draw.)

Fat hit: A shot in which the clubhead hits the ground in front of the ball. This considerably shortens the length of the flight.

Feedback: Information about the flight of the ball, the divot, the feeling at the moment of impact, etc. which helps a golfer improve.

Follow-through: The part of the swing from the moment of impact to the forward end position.

Forward movement: The part of the swing from the end of the backswing to the end of the follow-through.

Hook: A shot that starts out in the direction of the target and then veers off to the left.

Hosel: The cavity in the clubhead of an iron that encloses the shaft.

GLOSSARY

Late hit: A shot that occurs when the angle between the left arm and the shaft of the club dissolves very late.

Leading-edge: The lower front edge of the clubhead.

Lie of the club: The angle between the shaft of the club and the sole of the clubhead.

Loft: The angle between the clubface and a vertical line to the ground which lifts the ball into the air.

Pitch: A high approach shot.

Plane: A golf swing has several planes:
1. *The club plane* is defined by the lie of the club.
2. *The arm plane* is the angle of the left arm viewed from the side.
3. *The shoulder plane* is the angle created by the upper left and right sides of the shoulders during a swing, as viewed from the side.
  A plane is flat when it is oriented more horizontally, and it is steep when oriented more vertically.

Point of release: The moment during the downswing when the angle between the lower left arm and the club begins to widen, or increase.

Pronation: The rotation of the lower arm in the direction of the side of the thumb.

Pull: A ball that starts out to the left and then flies straight.

Push: A ball that starts out to the right and then flies straight.

Release: The moment at impact when the angle between the lower left arm and the club returns to zero degrees and the energy of the swing transfers to the follow-through.

Reverse pivot: A faulty body movement during the swing in which the player shifts his weight onto the wrong foot.

Sand wedge: A special club for the bunker designed so that the sole slides smoothly through the sand instead of burying itself. Because of its large loft, the sand wedge is also ideal for pitching.

Setup: An overall term for the grip, stance, position, and alignment.

Shank: A ball hit with the socket, or hosel, of the club, causing the ball to veer to the right or to the left.

Slice: A ball that starts out in the direction of the target and then veers to the right in the air.

Socket: See shank.

Supination: The rotation of the lower arm in the direction of the little finger.

Sweet spot: The ideal place to hit the ball because it is the point on the clubface where the perfect energy transfer to the ball takes place.

Target line: The straight line from the ball to the target.

Thin hit: A ball hit above its equator. The result is a flatter curve and no backspin.

Tilting: The rotation of the shoulders towards a steep plane (left shoulder too low, right shoulder too high).

Topping: Hitting the top of the ball with the bottom of the club.

Trailing edge: The lower, back edge of the clubhead.

Ulnar flexion: Flexing the wrists in the direction of the little finger.

Volar flexion: Flexing the wrists towards the palm of the hand.

Waggle: A movement made with the hands and lower arms before a shot that players use to get a feeling for the club and to be sure their hands are not clenched.

Wedge: A short club with a lot of loft. A pitching wedge has 52 degrees, a sand wedge has 56 degrees, and a loft wedge has 60 degrees.

INDEX

141

INDEX

Acknowledgments

Use of golf equipment: Bridgestone Sports Europe GmbH, Schwaben Market; Mizuno of Germany GmbH, Munich; Pro Shop of Öschberghof Golf Course and Club, Donaueschingen; Rolco Sport Products BV, Tilburg, The Netherlands

Photo shoot locations: Öschberghof Golf Course and Club, Donaueschingen; Neckartal Golf Club e.V., Ludwigsburg-Pattonville

Credits

Photos: HARDT Sportphoto Int., Hamburg, pp. 1, 2, 4–5 (4 photos), 6, 8–9 (Golf & Country Club at Hockenberg e.V., Seevetal), 20–21 (GC Adriatic, Cervia, Italy), 100–101 (Golf Course and Club of Lüdersburg Castle e.V., Lüdersburg by Lüneburg), 127, 134–135 (St. Eurach Course and Golf Club e.V., Iffeldorf), 136; Atelier G&M Köhler, Leonberg: all other photographs.

Artwork: CV&L, Kurt Dittrich, Miharbeit A. Schickert, all Wiesbaden.